PRAISE FOR
Knights in Training

"As a father seeking to raise a son in an environment that seems at times hostile to the idea of manhood, I found Heather's book both challenging and refreshing! I pray that the ten principles espoused in this book would by God's grace become normative for how we seek to raise our boys into men."

—Matt Chandler, author, lead pastor of the Village Church, president of the Acts 29 Church Planting Network

"I am so grateful to see a fresh perspective on an age-old quest: raising boys into men. Using the time-honored code of the knights, Heather reminds parents that not much has changed when it comes to raising the next generation of young men. Treat women with respect. Tell the truth. Be generous. Thanks, Heather! I needed that. We all need it."

—Heidi St. John, author, speaker, creator of thebusymom.com

"Chivalry does not have to die and civility does not have to be a lost art form, but the only way for these to make a comeback in society is to start in families and at home. Heather Haupt offers fascinating insight into the current state of boyhood and manhood, alongside a practical and fun guide for training our boys in the ways of courage, kindness, and honor. I'm inspired to raise my three boys to be modern-day knights who will love God, respect and serve others, and leave this world a better place than they found it."

—Erin Mohring, cofounder of the MOB Society and Raising Boys Ministries, writer at homewiththeboys.net

"Heather Haupt has written a much-needed guide for raising boys into men . . . Chivalry is all but dead, but Haupt's excellent book will tell parents how to bring it back to life!"

—John Rosemond, family psychologist, author of *Parenting by the Book*

KNIGHTS *in* TRAINING

TEN PRINCIPLES *for*

Raising Honorable, Courageous,

and Compassionate Boys

Heather Haupt

A TarcherPerigee Book

tarcherperigee

An imprint of Penguin Random House LLC
375 Hudson Street
New York, New York 10014

Most TarcherPerigee books are available at special quantity discounts
for bulk purchase for sales promotions, premiums, fund-raising, and
educational needs. Special books or book excerpts also can be created
to fit specific needs. For details, write: SpecialMarkets@
penguinrandomhouse.com.

ISBN 9780143130505

Printed in the United States of America
10 9 8 7 6 5 4 3 2 1

Book design by Katy Riegel

Contents

PART 1 ✦ The Boy-Raising Adventure

1. Charting a New Path   *3*

2. Why We Don't Want to Raise Typical Boys   *11*

3. Boys Are Different   *25*

PART 2 ✦ The Chivalry Challenge

4. Knights in Training:
   Stoking the Fires of a Lifelong Quest   *41*

5. Physical Training for the Quest   *54*

6. The Code: Love God   *71*

7. The Code: Obey   *89*

8. The Code: Stand Against Injustice   *108*

9. The Code: Protect the Weak   *122*

10. The Code: Respect Women   *139*

11. The Code: Don't Give Offense   *159*

12. The Code: Speak Truth   *180*

13. The Code: Be Generous   *198*

14. The Code: Persevere   *217*

15. The Code: Pursue Excellence   *237*

PART 3 ✛ Continuing the Quest

16. Raising Modern-Day Knights
    Is a Long-Term Quest   *253*

Appendices   *263*
Acknowledgments   *273*
Index   *275*

For my three knights-in-the-making,
Alexander, Keegan, and Treyton

{KNIGHT'S CODE OF CHIVALRY}

✠ *Love God with all your heart, soul, mind, and strength.*

✠ *Obey those in authority over you.*

✠ *Stand against injustice and evil.*

✠ *Defend the weak and protect them.*

✠ *Respect the honor of women.*

✠ *Refrain from wanton giving of offense.*

✠ *Speak the truth at all times.*

✠ *Be generous and willing to share.*

✠ *Persevere and finish the task at hand.*

✠ *Pursue excellence in all you do.*

✠ Part I

The Boy-Raising Adventure

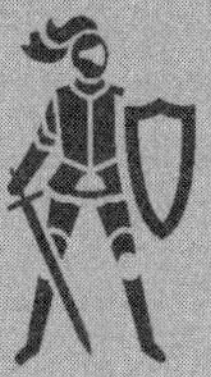

✛ CHAPTER I

Charting a New Path

ONE DAY, long ago at the *almost grown-up* age of twelve, I made my way to the neighborhood candy shop. A group of boys was loafing around and throwing barbs at one another. They were calling each other every variation of body parts and functions that you could dream up and laughing at their own supposed cleverness. I knew what came next. Cringing inside, I picked up my pace. As I passed them, their banter paused momentarily before altering direction. I was now the target, and the teasing took on an overt sexual nature. Some of them teased, while others looked the other way, perhaps embarrassed. Two of them started to follow as I ducked into the safety of the candy shop. The kind old man who ran the shop would not tolerate that kind of talk in his store and told the boys to leave. With an apathetic shrug they wandered off in search of new diversions.

We see these kinds of boys everywhere—the ones who

are rude and crude, the ones who find entertainment in picking on others, the ones who, for all of their bravado, become speechless and weak when someone needs to stand up against the bully. The entitlement mentality is firmly entrenched, resulting in teens doing what they please and behaving like tantrum-throwing toddlers when someone stands in their way. They expect life to be handed to them on a silver platter while they sit back and enjoy themselves.

Boys are increasingly disengaged, turned off to all that matters. Many struggle in school, preferring the allure of video games, and fewer are going to and graduating from college. Instead of boys eager for independence, more young men choose to stay home now than ever before, relying on parental support far longer than their female counterparts. Within this modern state of boyhood, mediocrity and apathy are the growing marks of manhood.

✦ Idealism to Fatalism

Most of us enter into parenthood with a sense of idealism. We hold a cute little baby and stare in wonder at his fresh skin, rosebud mouth, and perfect round ears. As his tiny fingers curl around ours, an unspoken resolve fills our heart—to raise this little one well, to raise a child who will make a difference in this world.

And then reality hits. If the sleepless nights or the unexplained crying that cannot be soothed does not cause doubt to set in, the first time your child throws a tantrum out in public just might. Maybe it happened when he pulled out all the toys after you had just tidied up or you caught him in a little white lie after working on truthfulness over and over again. You might have felt like throwing up the white flag of surrender as he races laps around you insisting that he is not tired at bedtime or magically disappears right after you ask him to help you with something. When they get wild and crazy, it can be tempting to calm and contain them with video games or a tablet.

We all agree: Parenting is not for the faint of heart. It takes dedication and a whole lot of consistency as we learn in a radical way to put our children's needs (not wants) above our own. It is easy to get tired and weary, because some days it is just inevitable. It can be tempting to ease up and allow our children to do things we said we would never let them do or to let bad behavior slide because we just do not want to deal with it at that moment.

Between the idealism of new parenthood and the drudgery of day-to-day parenting, fatalism can set in, and we begin to accept the cultural stereotypes about boys. We must not let this happen.

There are a lot of people talking about the problem. But where are the solutions? We all need practical ideas for inspiring this next generation of boys and changing the microculture in which our boys will grow up. We need a road map, if you will, pointing the way to go. Something that provides direction but also the flexibility to allow each family and each boy the ability to make the path his own. The aim of this book is to do just that—to give you a strategy and plan to inspire the imagination of young boys and lay the groundwork for creating a family and community culture that prepares our boys to thrive and make the world around them a better place.

Is it possible to raise these boys of ours to be confident and yet kind? Is it possible to capitalize on all the energy and drive of young boyhood to captivate their imagination as they are propelled toward adulthood?

Enter the world of knights. They've mesmerized boys ever since medieval times, when real ones roamed the land. My boys were no different. If it is possible to be both starry-eyed and stoically focused, this is how I would describe my boys when we first delved into the history of the Middle Ages. This is when I read about chivalry for the first time. What I learned surprised me. I had always thought of chivalry as merely how a man treats a woman. But it is far more than that. It is an entire code of conduct. As my boys waged imaginary battles all around me, I read and was filled with the vision of raising modern-day knights.

I desired to raise my boys to treat others with respect, to fight for what is right and good, to stand against injustice and evil, to defend and protect those who are weak. Although the culture at large increasingly demeans women, I wanted to raise strong sons who would show thoughtfulness and care, not only for the women they encounter each day but for *everyone*. I saw an opportunity to inspire my boys to seek to build one another up instead of tearing others down. In a *me*-focused culture, I wanted to emphasize loving God first and from there loving others. So as we learned about the *history* of the Middle Ages, we delved into *character development* too.

The deeper we delved, the more inspired my boys became. They wanted to emulate knights in every way. Why wouldn't they? A knight's life is full of adventure. Knights are respected and admired for their heroic bravery; they are called on in the time of need, and they rise up to rescue and help others.

This was my lightbulb moment! Why not "train" these boys to become knights? Whoops of delight and resolve met this announcement as they were eager to start. The training was rigorous (for little boys) and included daily running, archery practice, sword fights, stick horse rides to the park (in full armor—you should have seen the curious looks of our neighbors!), mock battles, and jousting practice. They even shined my silver because their armor and weapons consisted of cardboard, foam, and papier–mâché.

But we didn't stop there . . . Nope! In the name of raising modern-day knights, I introduced them to the idea of chivalry. As expected, my boys were drawn to this too, and so we took extra time in their knighthood training to include instructing, practicing, and rewarding chivalrous behavior. There are an amazing number of opportunities, even for young boys, to implement *the code* in their own lives.

They were to aspire to live out the following:

1. Love the Lord your God with your heart, soul, mind, and strength.
2. Obey those in authority over you.

3. Stand against injustice and evil.
4. Defend and protect the weak.
5. Respect and honor women.
6. Refrain from wanton offense.
7. Speak the truth at all times.
8. Be generous and willing to share.
9. Persevere and finish the task at hand.
10. Pursue excellence in all you do.

My boys love charts that show their progress, so we printed out "knight training charts" for the two older boys. Stars were bequeathed when I spotted heroic feats of chivalry. Soon I started to catch them stepping up and defending their baby brother against "injustice" (warring other brother) or racing out to open the car door for Aunt B. The boys were eager to carry groceries from the cart to the car and then into the house. I even saw the son who was struggling with lying, confess and speak the truth, even though it meant facing consequences—a true sign of bravery and strength.

Afterward, we had a dubbing ceremony in which the boys were each knighted by the king of the house. They were quite serious about it all, preparing the throne room and kneeling so reverently. Even the three-year-old slowed down from his frenzied running to watch and participate.

Long after we moved on from our initial foray into the Middle Ages, the boys were still eager to continue their knight training and grow in strength and valor.

I have come to realize that this training in chivalry was

only the beginning. We have revisited this challenge with more advanced training many times. We introduced more intense physical training by graduating from a suction-cup bow and arrow to a genuine kid's archery set and hay bale in the backyard. They comprehend the importance of the strength of character at a deeper level now than they did when we first introduced the challenge at the ages of three, four, and six years old. Now, six years later, they are excited to grow in strength and stature as they eagerly look forward to manhood. Our resolve to use this fabulous tool has only grown as they continue their journey of knights-in-the-making!

✢ Throwing Down the Gauntlet

As you progress through this book, the phrase *throwing down the gauntlet* will become very familiar. It refers to the medieval tradition of throwing down one's glove and challenging another to stand and defend himself or what he knows is true.

Right now I am issuing that challenge to you. I am throwing down the gauntlet, challenging you to step into your role to raise an honorable man. I am challenging you to raise a modern-day knight.

This chivalry challenge might make you uncomfortable at times. It will stretch you to live up to the integrity that you are challenging your son or sons to pursue. But it is entirely worth it because *they* are worth it.

Yes, there are problems in our culture. But we do not need to be consumed with fear or fatalism. It *is* possible to raise boys entirely different from the cultural norm. So be a warrior, not a worrier! Be fiercely loyal and dedicated to raising your boys up.

Now, let's tackle this challenge together!

✢ CHAPTER 2

Why We Don't Want to Raise Typical Boys

EMBRACING THE CHIVALRY CHALLENGE allows us to tackle the problems of modern-day masculinity head on. We do not have to raise a typical modern-day boy. But to do this, we need to have a clear idea of what we do *not* want as well as a vision for what we *do* want our boys to become in order to chart a course that prepares our sons to become the men that *they* really want to become—men who are respected and strong, tender and considerate.

Let us take an honest look at the state of modern-day boyhood and explore what it looks like to reverse this trend. It will take thoughtfulness on our part as we assess how we are parenting our children (or not parenting them) and whether this lines up with our long-term goals.

✦ We Promote Civility and Politeness

No matter what anyone else appears to be doing, or not doing, we promote civility and politeness in our homes. These lessons present themselves in the everyday moments of ordinary days.

A few years ago, a friend came into town with his wife and eight-year-old son. We arranged to meet up with them, bringing our same-aged boy. As we drove across town, our son talked excitedly about the opportunity to meet a new friend.

Unfortunately, he was in for a big disappointment. After sitting down at our table, the other boy promptly pulled out his iPad. In an attempt to help this boy feel at ease, my son asked him what he had done since arriving in Arizona. The boy mumbled something about swimming at the resort without even bothering to look up. As he put on his head-phones, his father chided him.

He unplugged the headphones, casting a sullen look toward his father. In response to further questions, he gave a few one-word responses and simply switched over to play-ing some kind of game.

My son learned that even when we are polite and friendly, it is not always reciprocated. I left resolved to be mindful to watch my own children and help them develop social awareness and courtesy toward others. The other boy's parents were not bad people; in fact, they were quite friendly. But they were not helping their son develop the skills he needed to make friends or be sympathetic.

When we think of the typical modern-day boy, we often think of boys who are sullen and bored, rude and crude. At least that is what we see in the shows and movies we watch, and it is often the behavior of the young people around us.

Of course, lack of civility certainly is not only a boy problem; it is growing increasingly systemic.[1] As we walk into this brave new world transformed by online interactions and instant everything, we must set the example of what it means to pursue civil discourse and work to shift the pendulum back toward the realm of civility.

What ever happened to being polite? Many parents these days have lost their way when it comes to training their children to be polite. We hear more *gimmes* rather than *please* and *thank yous*. It is cool to rag on others and tear them down with constant teasing instead of challenging or encouraging them. Our kids have lost the perception and ability of how to treat people whether by showing respect and deference toward their elders, looking people in the eye when talking, taking turns, or empathizing with those around them.

---

1. Rebecca A. Clay, "That's Just Rude," *Monitor on Psychology* 44, no. 10 (2013): 34. Available at apa.org/monitor/2013/11/rude.aspx.

✴ We Teach Our Boys to Define Themselves by Virtue Rather Than Potty Humor or Sexual Innuendo

When they were little, one of my boys could say something as simple as *poop*, and his brothers would burst into fits of unadulterated giggles and outright guffaws. It seems to be something hardwired into all little boys and manifests itself around the age of three.

This fact makes sense. In the midst of potty training, boys who adore all things gross and have that inborn desire to *push the envelope*, get a rush out of talking about gross things and feeling just a little bit naughty.

However, there used to be cultural restraints on potty humor. For example, do not talk about body parts or body functions at the dinner table, in front of Mom (or other ladies), at school, at church, etc. But these restraints appear to have all but ended. In the media's push for profit, crass humor has become an increasing mainstay, an easy way to get a laugh.

Children's media is not the only place where potty humor prevails. In our desperate attempts to get boys into books and end the "gender reading gap," a plethora of potty humor books have been churned out. One blogger promises, "Despite the ridiculous plot, these are genuine chapter books that, gross or not, count as reading. Cringe and bear it and you might just get your kid reading." But do we really need to resort to bribing our boys with books like *The Day My Butt Went Psycho, Captain Underpants and the Perilous Plot of Professor Poopypants,* or *Zombie Butts from Uranus?*[2]

The short answer is no. I will take up this topic later.

So What's the Big Deal with Fart Jokes?

When we fail to place boundaries or restraints and instead fill boys' minds with even more unrestrained crass humor through the books we give them or the shows they watch, they may not learn the necessary self-regulation skills to know when to turn it off. Boys lose the ability to read situations and take the feelings of others into account. Good boys find themselves in the confusing situation of hurting other children when they are actually trying to connect and laugh together.

What happens when little boys with unrestrained potty mouths become teenagers? The talk becomes sexual—and oftentimes directed toward those around them. You have situations in movies such as *17 Again,* in which kids are making sexual jokes about their friend's mother—for laughs. We have boys egging each other on and engaging in "Flip-up Fridays" where they aim to flip up a girl's skirt for a peek and a laugh.

We see teenage boys like Jared Grumney become a viral

---

2. Maria Mora, http://www.sheknows.com/parenting/articles/993695/gross-books
-that-little-kids-love.

Twitter sensation because so many other young men could identify with him when he used poetry to complain about girls, writing that he thought they were pretty until they rudely refused to shower with him or text him nudes.

If this is a typical modern-day boy who graduated from potty jokes to sexual innuendos and trying to guilt girls into sending him nude photographs, then we need to stand strong and say, "No, we don't want to raise a *typical boy.*"

✦ We Resist the *Entitlement* Mentality

Entitlement is reaching epidemic proportions. It is easy to spot, within other people's children at least.

Take Ethan Couch, the wealthy teen who showed no remorse after killing four people while driving intoxicated. He was let off on a light sentence because his lawyer claimed he was not responsible for his actions due to "affluenza"—a sense that a young person cannot comprehend the consequences of his actions because of financial privilege.

While this is an extreme case, the reality is that most of middle-class American kids struggle with an entitlement mentality to some degree or another.

Kristen Welch, author of *Raising Grateful Kids in an Entitled World* mentions the following five signs of entitlement. Do you recognize any of them in your own children?

I want it now.

I don't want to have to work for it.

I don't have to clean up my mess.

I want it because everyone else has it.

I expect you to fix all my problems.[3]

Entitlement is linked to narcissism, and researchers have seen a steady and dramatic increase in narcissism among college students over the last thirty to forty years. Narcissism is on the rise, and empathy levels are plummeting.[4]

Parents need to nip narcissism in the bud and say no to the encroaching entitlement mentality. We can do this by recognizing the crippling effect that this kind of thinking has on our children and how prevalent it is in our society. Then we need to respond by refusing some of our children's wants, placing limits in their lives, and teaching them the value of hard work. These changes will help our boys authentically engage with real people and real work.

---

3. Kristen Welch, "5 Signs Kids Are Struggling with Entitlement," *We Are THAT Family*, December 18, 2013. Available at wearethatfamily.com/2013/12/5-signs -kids-are-struggling-with-entitlement.

4. J. M. Twenge and J. D. Foster, "Birth Cohort Increases in Narcissistic Personality Traits among American College Students, 1982–2009," *Social Psychological and Personality Science* 1 (2010): 99–106. S. H. Konrath, E. H. O'Brien, and C. Hsing, "Changes in Dispositional Empathy in American College Students over Time: A Meta-Analysis," *Personality and Social Psychology Review* 15 (2011): 180–98.

✠ We Help Our Boys Engage

Modern notions of boyhood involve a boy with his face in a smartphone or tablet. The image of boys zoning out playing video games is not a new phenomenon. But technology is more readily available than ever and hawked to kids (and their parents) straight out of the womb. Twenty-five years ago, parents had to find ways to entertain children on long car trips; now it is not uncommon to see screens in SUVs and minivans to keep kids occupied and distracted on simple trips across town and to use phones to keep our kids quiet at restaurants.

While it may seem hard for parents to imagine, successful boyhood must involve the near-elimination of such devices. The late Steve Jobs and a host of tech giants from companies such as Google, Apple, Yahoo!, and eBay all have one thing in common—they create tech-free environments for their kids. Although they create the tech tools that are revolutionizing our world, they recognize the danger of putting such tools in young hands because of how they inhibit social and academic engagement and stunt innovation and creativity. These tech visionaries are establishing screen-free space at home and choosing technology free schools. They do so not to hold their children back but rather to allow them to develop the skills needed to engage with their world and become the innovators of tomorrow.

One of the main dangers with technology is that it deadens interest in other activities and can be highly addictive. Putting parameters in place and watching for signs of addiction early can be very helpful. Psychologist Richard Freed says that we must "recognize that children, with their developing brains, are highly vulnerable to today's advanced gaming technologies which are designed to be difficult to put down."[5]

Given the nature of technology, education is an obvious area in which an increasing number of boys are disengaging. The tech-free schools that the elite in this country are choosing for their kids embody a dramatically different educational philosophy from many traditional schools. They emphasize intellectual development beyond the worksheets and flashcards and provide an experience-rich, problem-solving approach to education in the early years.

Savvy families who do not have access to these kinds of schools are instead setting limits on their children's screen-time, creating schedules so their children have a shot at a relaxed childhood, working for reforms within the schools in their areas, or even opting to homeschool.

What are the long-term effects of tech-drugged boys? Aside from a widening gap in reading between boys and girls and a corresponding drop in overall school performance, we see significant changes during the college years. While the number of men pursuing a college education has remained consistent in the last fifty years, there has been

---

5. Richard Freed, "What One Boy's Story Tells Us about Video Game Addiction," *Huffington Post*, February 19, 2016. Available at huffingtonpost.com/richard-freed/what-one-boys-story-tells-us-about-video-game-addiction_b_9238744.html.

more than a 20 percent drop in the number of male college graduates. As a result, their financial earning potential takes a hit, which impacts their ability to obtain financial independence going into adulthood.[6]

✦ We Prepare Our Boys for Independence

The decrease in men graduating from college and the increase in those disengaging from reality altogether appear to coincide with other signs pointing to the fact that many millennial men are finding themselves adrift, having failed to launch.

Dependence on Mom and Dad is a growing trend among young adults, men in particular. A 2015 Pew Research Center analysis reveals that only 63 percent of millennial men (eighteen to thirty-four years old) are independent from their parents compared to 72 percent of women, and unemployment rates among these men remain high.[7] There is a growing number of young men who simply are not interested in seeking work at all. They are aimlessly drifting—no passion, no direction, and somehow able to coast by relying on others to take care of them—initially by their parents and then sometimes by wives or girlfriends.

---

6. National Center for Education Statistics, "Table 310. Degrees Conferred by Degree-Granting Institutions, by Level of Degree and Sex of Student: Selected Years, 1869–70 through 2021–22," Digest of Education Statistics. Available at nces.ed.gov/programs/digest/d12/tables/dt12_310.asp.

7. Richard Fry, "More Millennials Living with Family Despite Improved Job Market," Pew Research Center, July 29, 2015. Available at pewsocialtrends.org/2015/07/29/more-millennials-living-with-family-despite-improved-job-market.

During these times when "adulting" has become a scourge and prolonging adolescence all the rage, we must take the initiative to prepare our children for future independence.

The drive for independence used to be the mark of masculinity, and the aim of this book is to give parents a strategy for fostering this once again in our boys. Although I used to tease my sons about staying little forever, I knew, just as other parents do, that they are meant to become men, making their way in the world and starting a family of their own. Our goal as parents is to prepare them to *fly* when it comes time to leave the roost.

✦ Let's Work Toward a Solution

Although you and I may not be called to make drastic changes on a large-scale cultural or political level, we can make a huge difference in our homes and even in our local communities.

The biggest actions we can take to reverse these trends in modern boyhood are to recognize societal influences and make the radical decision to remake our family's culture and, if possible, to create a micro-culture in our communities where these stated values are emphasized.

✠ Mindful Media Consumption

We begin this work by becoming mindful media consumers and teaching our children to adopt this mind-set as well. Setting limits on media use is one aspect. We also teach them to discern the messages coming through the TV and movies we watch and the video games that they play. Media has a profound effect on how we think and behave. If that were not true, marketers would not be spending millions on advertisements and product placements.

We want to be aware of the messages being communicated about what it means to be a boy and a man. Males of all ages are often depicted as gross, uncouth, lazy, and stupid creatures. Being an underachiever is a badge of honor. Dads are portrayed as boring, bumbling fools. It is no wonder, then, that boys do not want to grow up. We need to recognize these messages in shows, movies, books, or even commercials and then talk to our kids about them. Limiting exposure to these kinds of harmful messages is key too.

Take *The Lego Movie*, for instance. Emmet is a relaxed dude who simply goes to his boring job every day. He spends his free time watching shows like *Honey, Where Are My Pants* (vacuous) and mooning the photocopy machine (immature). While he does rise to the occasion to try to become the hero, he manages to do so only because his female sidekick does most of the thinking and much of the rescuing for him. After our boys watched the movie, we talked about it. However, we did not purchase it because this was not a message we wanted our boys to hear over and over again. *Frozen* is another movie we limit. Why? From a male standpoint alone, we see the men in the movie portrayed as bumbling and lazy or power-hungry and evil.[8]

If we want our boys to grow up to be loving, wonderful fathers, we need to give them positive role models, and these are increasingly hard to come by. Our family collects older movies that still portray men as smart and caring, men who protect and provide for their families, men who are respected by their wives because we hope that someday they will meet amazing women and step into their role of raising their own children.

Sometimes vintage is just better. While the new *Lone Ranger* movie has amazing cinematography and effects, it features a far different Long Ranger from the original TV series. This new version is the stereotypical bumbling and naive fool who needed the "not all there" Tonto (also an affront to the original) to somehow miraculously rescue him. The original Lone Ranger, by contrast, was as courageous as he was kind and honest. And the original Tonto embodied the beauty of teamwork with his ingenuity and faithfulness. Those characters are true role models for boys!

---

8. While I love movies with strong female characters, it saddens me when they have to put a man down to make a woman look strong and capable. It is possible to have a strong female lead without having to denigrate men.

✝ Establish Family Culture

Placing limits on media consumption is important for family life too. Richard Freed, author of *Wired Child* writes, "Obsessive use of video games, social media, and texting are depriving kids of shared family moments, an interest in school, and other vital childhood experiences."

We can limit these harmful effects for both our children and ourselves when we make family life a priority. Restore family mealtimes and make relationships a priority over work, school, extracurriculars, social media, and anything else that might be keeping us apart.

Safeguard our children's time so they can process and internalize what they are learning.

As we strengthen family relationships and really start to talk about the issues of our day, we can establish a family culture that can overcome negative outside influences. It is a slow process, but we *can* work toward reversing these societal trends and creating a better future.

It is time to fully engage. In our high-speed world, it is easy to want to outsource our parenting. Schools can be a wonderful tool, but it is unfair and foolish to expect a teacher with twenty to forty students to take care of the entirety of our children's academic, character, and behavior development. The foundation for that must come from the home. Embracing the idea of knights in training reminds us of our role to train, and it helps our boys understand their role to learn and prepare for the adventures to come.

✛ CHAPTER 3

Boys Are Different

I NEVER WORRIED about being a boy mom. In the weeks preceding my first son's arrival, I waddled around the nursery inspecting the stacks of freshly laundered onesies, tucking in his crib sheet, and contemplating the adventure ahead. With a smug grin, I threw up a prayer of thanks for my tomboy ways as a child. As one of three girls, I was as close to a boy as my dad would get. I caught snakes, placed cicada shells in other girls' hair—just to hear them scream— and could be found most days hanging upside down from a tree or running atop the cinderblock walls in my neighborhood. Yep, I was going to rock this boy mom thing.

Or so I thought.

Three sons later, there was no doubt in my mind: Boys are different. My friends with girls post delightful pictures of their daughters dressing up and having tea parties. Meanwhile my three boys engage in mud battles and smear clods in the trees, the walls, and even on the sides of the house.

They also do not stop moving, unless they are sleeping. And my job is to keep them alive. Period. Come four o'clock in my home, I always boot the boys outside to burn off energy. Everyone's survival and sanity depends on this. In our blisteringly hot summers, when they cannot go outside, they take to playing football in the house while I make dinner. Of course, they had to invent a way to play without the actual football because I outlawed ball throwing inside.

And then, the wrestling. These three boys of mine wrestle. Fierce looks overtake their adorable young faces, looks so fierce it is a challenge for me to decipher when they are just having fun and when it has slipped over into a real fight. I just do not get it. On one particular day when I went to intervene, my husband pulled me back.

"They're just having fun, Heather."

"What? No, they are trying to kill one another. We need to work on getting along here," I resolutely replied.

"This *is* getting along."

I still do not think I believed my husband until I remembered back to the time his parents had come to visit, and I caught him and his dad wrestling. Yes, two grown men, wrestling like young boys.

But will they ever become civilized, I wondered.

The answer I have learned over the years is yes. But it looks different from what I had expected. I simply needed to understand and then embrace their differences. Although there is so much men and women have in common,

how we express thoughts or feelings and how we are motivated can oftentimes be very different.

With this I mind, here are six things we need to understand about our boys before we jump into knight training.

✱ 1. Boys Thrive on Adventure

Boys are drawn to the thrill of adventure. Although some
boys are more cautious than others, they all relish at least
the *idea* of embarking on some kind of adventure. As long
as they are not drugged by electronics, most boys are ready
to explore the world around them. They are drawn to adventure stories and action-packed movies.

Cowboy stories, in particular, enthrall my boys, just as
they have past generations. They do not just want to watch
adventure; they want to live it. There are many days when I
see a boy running, stick horse in hand, to round up those
outlaws. When given the freedom and flexibility, young
boys frequently relive these adventures through their pretend play.

While I did not particularly care for superhero movies,
cartoons, or books and attempted to shield my sons from
what I felt was shameless and excessive marketing, the boys
naturally gravitated toward the likes of Superman, Spider-
Man, and Batman. It took them only ten minutes at a
friend's home to locate the superhero toys and begin making laps around the house lost in surprisingly accurate
imaginative play, despite my attempts to shelter them.

Risk is an essential element of adventures. And boys are natural risk takers, whether it is leaning over the railing of a tall building, tying a rope to the back of a bike and pulling along a friend on a skateboard, or experimenting with aluminum foil in the electrical outlets. They relish the element of danger and daring these activities afford. My dad told me about the time his uncle promised him that eating his lima beans would help him fly. At dinner that night, he pounded down a plateful of those nasty beans before setting out to the backyard with his brother where they decided to test the theory by jumping off the fence. The result—a broken arm, broken dreams, and a great story!

In addition to taking risks, boys want an audience. Research backs this up. During one study, students were handed rings and told to complete a ring toss. No other directions were given and they were left alone to complete the task. Women would walk up to the target, dropping the rings directly down. The men, on the other hand, would take a few steps back to give themselves a little bit of a challenge. They tried the experiment again, except that this time two other people of the same gender were in the room. The women did nothing different, again walking over and dropping the rings onto the target. But instead of standing a few feet back as before, the men moved to the other side of the room before dramatically attempting the ring toss, demonstrating the fact that it was not the accuracy of hitting the target that mattered to them, but the bravado in undertaking a greater challenge. Because of the value they place on risk, the presence of other men pushed them to take even greater risks.

✛ 2. Boys Want to Be Strong

"Look at my muscles," Ethan shouted to anyone and everyone who would listen, as he hiked up his sleeves and proceeded to flex. There is a desire within most boys to be
strong. This often manifests itself in bursts of activity to
showcase their budding strength. Most guys just get it, but
mothers and female teachers can often bristle at the ma-
chismo displayed or fret about the potential for destruction.

This is not entirely unfounded. Boys can be like bulls in
a china shop, ticking time bombs ready to explode. They
make big movements and love to test their strength. Just as
they long for adventure, they long to have the strength to
be the hero of the story. This is not only OK but should be
fostered and encouraged. We need to resist the urge to roll
our eyes and embrace this nearly universal trait in the male
half of the population. Instead of trying to minimize the
importance of physical strength or to divert them to more
peaceful and sedentary activity, we need to channel their
energy, their desire to prove their strength into productive
ends.

Occasionally a bagger at the grocery store will offer to
help me out to the car and load up my groceries. While I
appreciated the help when I had three little boys, aged three
and under, I no longer need the help. Why? I have three sets
of amazing muscles ready and willing to outdo one another
in carrying grocery bags to the car and then into the house.
There are countless ways for them to help, and they jump at

the chance to show off their muscles because they love the admiration and thanks we give them when they help. Choosing to view their obsession with strength as a natural part of their design opens up many opportunities for us to work together. They learn, even at a young age, to use their strength to help others.

Why do boys want big muscles? Why do they want to be strong? It is part of what typifies masculinity. It provides a feeling of self-sufficiency, a feeling of safety, and yes, possibly even a feeling of power. It is something that sets men apart from women. We do not need to fear this, but rather celebrate male strength (in whatever capacity our particular boys have been given) and encourage it toward good and honorable ends, to civilize this raw strength. As Brett McKay puts it, "What good are intellectual achievements and moral principles, if those who hold and cultivate them are subdued by those who care nothing for these higher values?"[1] Strength forms the nucleus of manliness, making all other uniquely manly virtues possible.

✝ 3. Boys Need to Move

The reality is that everyone needs to move. It is essential for neurological and emotional development as well as physical health. However, in a culture that prizes the idea of kids

---

1. Brett McKay, "Why Every Man Should Be Strong," *Art of Manliness*, August 13, 2014. Available at artofmanliness.com/2014/08/13/why-every-man-should-be -strong.

sitting still all the time, our wiggly young boys suffer the most, which is precisely why so many little boys struggle in school. If they move, they are punished for not behaving. Yet when they do not have ample time to move, parents and educators often end up with even more discipline and defiance issues or boys who simply shut down and disengage from learning and the world around them altogether. It is entirely possible for boys to sit still; we just need to be mindful of how often we are expecting them to do so and be sure that they have plenty of opportunities to move around.

Diane is the mother of nine. That's right, *nine* children. Right after I had my third son and was entirely overwhelmed, I cornered her and asked her what the secret was to raising these crazy and very active boys. Without missing a beat, she responded, "Labor, heavy labor." Her husband was a farmer and the boys were involved at an early age working the farm. The result of that hard labor is evident today; her adult sons are hardworking men who are leaders in their various professional fields.

Another mother of many boys, Heather, voiced similar sentiments. She did not live on a farm, but required her sons to swim a certain number of laps in the backyard pool before they sat down to homework and before they could just relax and play later in the day. This physical outlet was a sanity saver not only for her but also for her boys.

My sons are your typical busy and active boys. Experience has taught me to get strategic when it comes to helping them sit in one place. If I know I am going somewhere

where they will need to sit still, or where they will need to conduct themselves with quiet respect, such as the library or a museum, I am sure to have them spend some time roughhousing or playing hard in the backyard beforehand to get the wiggles out of their systems.

✝ 4. Boys Need to Know Why

There is something fascinating about boys and motivation. Girls are typically motivated by relationships—with their teachers, parents, and friends. From an early age, it is easier for them to empathize with an adult perspective and understand it. They are typically hardwired to want to please the teacher or other adults in their life.

Boys, on the other hand, are motivated by competition and other boys rather than adults. When a boy defies authority, says something that is rude or crude, or engages in risky behavior, he does it to gain kudos and credibility from the other boys. A girl who defies authority will not elevate her standing with her girlfriends.[2]

For a boy to override his impulse to behave in a rude, crude, or dangerous way, he needs not only to know why but also to have internalized that why. He needs to connect behavior, belief, and internal character with real-life situations. Knowing the why helps him not only accept training and direction but embrace it. Appealing to his rational side

---

2. Leonard Sax, *Boys Adrift* (New York City: Basic Books, 2007), p. 25.

is far more effective than badgering him. Armed with the why, he can connect to his emerging manhood and inner strength, and he will be more likely to resist the temptation to do stupid things in the quest to fit in with the guys.

Nutrition is an area where the why was important to my family. But instead of just telling my kids that they would eat what we put in front of them (which they will because that is a given in our home), I spent quite a bit of time teaching them how eating poorly impedes their body's ability to function well. As a result, they made their own decision to eat what I call "winning foods," foods that propel them forward toward victory.

On a subsequent trip to the grocery store, my boys excitedly talked about the winning foods they hoped I would purchase. My triumph was complete when my middle guy specifically asked for broccoli. He begged for it, in fact. In his excitement about the super healing power of vitamin C, he forgot his dislike of this particular veggie. It still took them a while to fully acquire a taste for some of the healthy foods I provided, but they were totally convinced that it was worth eating and began challenging each other to "train their taste buds."

✷ 5. Boys Need a Vision

The idea of a role model is not a cliché. People become whom they admire. Boys long to be the hero, not just because of the adventure and not just to prove their strength.

No, boys want to make a difference in this world and to do so in the thrilling and action-packed ways they were designed to do it. Connecting our boys with heroes from the past fills their mind with a vision of how they can become the heroes of both the present and the future.

Heroes come in many shapes and sizes. Of course, modern boys are drawn to fictional heroes like the latest Marvel wonder, and those characters have their place. However, we need also to connect boys to the heroes of history—real men who overcame all kinds of setbacks, weaknesses, and failure to become people who responded with strength and dignity when the need arose and made a difference in the lives of those around them, altering the very course of history.

These men include George Washington, Davy Crockett, Martin Luther King Jr., Robert E. Lee, and Frederick Douglass. From the Middle Ages, there are the legends of King Arthur and his knights of the Round Table, the heroic deeds of Alfred the Great, the boldness of William Wallace, and the loyalty and epic bravery of William Marshal.

Be careful about the biographies you choose. A disturbing trend in recent decades is to cut heroes down to size—to find the flaws (which all humans possess) and focus inordinate attention on them. Children's books are increasingly taking a mocking tone toward great men like George Washington and some books about knights reduce them all to crude and violent creatures with no morals or class.

The antihero that is so common in pop culture is a person who lacks heroic qualities such as courage, kindness, and most notably moral goodness. Presumably, these antiheroes are currently popular because, as one young person put it, "Antiheroes liberate us. They reject societal constraints and expectations imposed upon us." They celebrate and elevate selfishness and seek to obliterate any guilt about it. I'm not suggesting that we whitewash history, but we need to resist the nihilistic urge to fail to see real virtue in life and to emasculate all of our heroes. Yes, heroes are ordinary people, but they courageously embody extraordinary valor by facing a problem head-on and selflessly seeking to help others.

✠ 6. Boys Need Expectations

Stephen Covey, in his famous book *The 7 Habits of Highly Effective People*, writes: "Treat a man as he is and he will remain as he is. Treat a man as he can and should be and he will become as he can and should be." Boys will rise to the expectations others place on them, whether low or high. Setting high expectations starts early when we expect all our children to contribute to the family not only by tidying their own room but also by doing chores that benefit the entire household. This gives our children a sense of belonging and develops the value of work.

Recently, I packed my three boys and little girl into the car for a trip to the Dallas Museum of Art. As we walked into each exhibit hall, a look of wariness came over the security guards, and they hovered nearby to make sure my curious kids did not touch anything. These boys, who had goofed off as we attempted to load up the car, were now walking with measured steps at the museum, notebooks in hand to sketch their favorite scenes. You would not believe the number of comments we received. "However did you manage to get your boys inside an art museum? How did you get them to remain calm?" The answer lies in my expectations.

I am all for letting boys run around like crazy hooligans in the backyard. They need to have the flexibility to burn off steam, to climb trees, to engage in imaginary battles. But these boisterous boys of mine also know how to conduct themselves with quiet respect in the library, at church, or even at the art museum.

This starts with setting expectations in my home and enforcing them. It doesn't happen by chance. I needed to be diligent, patient, and determined in our children's early years. I must take up the mantle of leadership as the parent to guide, direct, and train my children. It took weeks of getting down at their level each and every time we entered the library. We would discuss appropriate and inappropriate behavior before stepping inside. It required continued discussions about these expectations as three active boys learned the discipline of self-regulation. But those discussions paved the way for the ease we now enjoy when attending the symphony or visiting a museum and the commendations they receive for their courteous behavior.

Of course, setting expectations is a work in progress and takes some humility as a parent. Many years ago, my boys and I joined a family music class. The teacher focused on making music fun, interactive, and movement rich. My boys loved it! As the tempo became livelier, their dancing became frenetic, then morphed into tackling. I made a few attempts to break it up, but gave up, thinking that boys would be boys. In reality, their behavior was disruptive and out of hand. Soon the rest of the boys in the class had jumped into the melee. It was a painful moment when the teacher told me that my boys needed to change or they would be asked to leave. I swallowed my pride and my boys learned self-control in that context.

As parents set expectations in small ways, day by day, they create a family culture that communicates and follows through with what it means to be not only part of our family but also part of a community and society. They learn what it means to become a man whose strength is carefully balanced by his character and the quality of his inward soul in the decisions he makes when no one is watching.

✢ Embracing Boyhood

Embracing boyhood in all of its exuberance and energy can be quite a challenge to parents who crave a peaceful and organized life. It is easier in the short term to limit their access to active play and try to curb their appetite for all risk taking. But that shortcut truncates male development and fails to recognize the beauty and strength of their budding masculinity. Take boys as they are and provide them a context to grow into the strong, self-determined heroes they aspire to be—this is what knight training is all about. So let us embrace their love for adventure, their muscle, and their need to move, and cultivate those traits within the framework of heroic stories and high expectations. It is time for knight training!

✠ Part 2

The Chivalry Challenge

✛ CHAPTER 4

Knights in Training: Stoking the Fires of a Lifelong Quest

Since it is so likely that [children] will meet cruel enemies,
let them at least have heard of brave knights and heroic
courage.   —*C. S. Lewis*

HOW DID A YOUNG BOY become a knight in the Middle Ages? It started early. He would begin duties as a page at the age of six or seven. Helping serve food, running errands, and cleaning were the unglamorous duties of a page. During this time, the ladies of the manor trained him in manners and civility. Occasionally, academic lessons were included. A page was issued a dagger and wooden sword and shield to practice the art of war in the castle yard with the other boys. In his spare moments, he would sneak away to watch the older boys train, eagerly anticipating his own future feats.

Around the age of fourteen, a boy would become squire to a knight. At this point, the boy would be the personal assistant to this knight, keeping the older man's armor in top condition and caring for the horses as he learned physically to master the art of war. In the event of a battle, the squire accompanied his knight to the battlefield to make sure the knight's needs were met. He might pull him from the battlefield if wounded or get him a fresh lance, if possible.

By age twenty-one, most squires were ready for promotion to knighthood. At this pivotal point, a squire permanently left boyhood behind and charged full-speed into manhood. In ideal circumstances, an elaborate ceremony was held. The squire would bathe (which was a rare event in those days) and spend the night in the church praying and pledging to serve God. He would then present himself dressed in white to the king or lord of the castle. The knight-to-be would pledge loyalty to the king, be dubbed, and receive his golden spurs. Surprisingly, this dubbing was not a gentle tap on both shoulders with the sword, but rather a hard blow that oftentimes left bruises. It signified the solemnity of his pledge to serve the king (or lord) and to live a chivalric life. Oftentimes, as we see in the story of the Kitchen Knight, this act of knighting was performed in the context of battle when valor was observed. If a lord needed more soldiers for an upcoming battle, he would perform an impromptu knighting ceremony before setting out.

There was nothing soft about the life of a page, squire, or knight. His purpose was training for battle. Neglect that preparation, and one would not last long on the battlefield. This required strict training of the mind as well as training of the body.

What, then, is chivalry?
Such a difficult, tough,
and very costly thing to learn
that no coward ventures to take it on.
—THE HISTORY OF WILLIAM MARSHAL

These words from *The History of William Marshal* communicate the mystique and wonder behind chivalric ideals. Few points in history have inspired future generations as much as the lore and history surrounding the knights of the Middle Ages. We are swept into the drama of an age long gone, but one that, no matter how brutal, still holds a mesmerizing draw. Why? Because the core principles are timeless. Good and evil exist, and we innately realize our need for selfless people who will stand against evil and protect the innocent, who will promote what is good, fair, and true. This war between good and evil exists in our very own hearts and is the reason the whole idea of chivalry came about in the first place.

This Code of Chivalry, which was never clearly delineated as a list of rules, was actually more of a set of underlying principles that permeated the narratives told about knights and were seamlessly woven into the training and very fabric of how they lived. It was deeply and unconsciously understood, much like later patriotic ideals in America.

The inspiration for the aspects of the Code of Chivalry included here comes directly from the French epic poem *Song of Roland*. It provides one of the earliest and most definitive pictures of chivalry. It is a riveting account of the importance of the character developed by chivalry and how steely resolve and inner strength plays out in life.

This poem was sung by troubadours for hundreds of years and eventually written down in the late eleventh century, when the notions of chivalry were becoming increasingly defined and more clearly taught to up-and-coming knights.

By the thirteenth century, the ideas of chivalry were well established and guided the elite and warrior classes. Geoffroi de Charny gives us the most authentic and complete manual on the day-to-day living out of chivalry because, unlike others who wrote on the topic, de Charny lived the life of a valorous knight until his death at the Battle of Poitiers. He writes not of a frivolous, shallow form of manners but rather of an intense way of living that required a man to give his all to his calling and to pursue that calling with a ferocity that set him apart from others. He was to discipline his mind and his body. This vocation was a holy calling, almost on par with that of a clergyman. Chivalry was not an optional value for the knight but rather intricately intertwined with his very identity. Those who strayed were passionately challenged to return to the ideal. Young boys training to become knights were immersed in this way of living from an early age.

De Charny wrote on the subject of chivalry because knighthood in the France of his day was unraveling. Decaying character was impacting the culture. Knights were both feared and openly mocked because of their wicked reputations and unchecked appetites for violence and power. They used their power to exploit innocent people. They gave way to base appetites leading them to violence and power grabs, or alternately toward cowardice, immorality, laziness, and greed. De Charny's book was a call for knights to return to a higher standard. He clearly communicated that a knight could and ought to know that the highest goals for a man to aspire to was to be a man of worth. He recognized that "if a man were sufficiently intelligent but not a man of worth, his intelligence would be turned wholly to evil."[1] He proclaimed that we need the ideals of chivalry not only to counteract the evil *out there* but also to check the bent toward evil inside each of us as individuals.

✛ The Challenge

I am writing now because we are at a similar crossroads. Violence and incivility are on the rise, and boys seem lost and adrift more than ever. This book is a call to return to the ideal. It is a call to celebrate boys and men for who they were designed to be and set them on a trajectory to take up the mantle of chivalry once again to restore order, dignity, and virtue to our communities. It is a call to parents to embody these ideals and pass them on to their children. This book provides a guide to do just that as you help your boys become all they were meant to be.

1. Geoffroi de Charny, *A Knight's Own Book of Chivalry* (Philadelphia: University of Pennsylvania Press, 2005), pp. 80–81.

You can do that through engaging the imagination and exposing them to the stories of knights, and then encouraging them to bring these stories into their play. You will begin to engage in regular conversations about the chivalric ideals and help them pursue hands-on application. Most important, you will not give up. Just as a knight's training encompassed most of his childhood, we recognize that we are in this for the long haul.

✟ The Role of Books and the Imagination

It was Christmas morning, and we were anticipating the opening of gifts just as much as the kids. My husband and I knew that we would be learning about the Middle Ages after the Christmas break, so we suggested medieval gift ideas to the grandparents. Tucked under the Christmas tree that year was a toy castle and several figurines to go with it as well as a toy battering ram and catapult that actually worked. The grown men could not wait to get their hands on that one. Squeals of delight resounded when the knights, horses, siege weapons, and castle were unwrapped.

Noticing the eagerness of the grown men to play with the weapons, the boys zeroed in on those. They are, after all, *boys*. Weapons have a special allure. I noticed however that their pretend play hardly resembled the accuracy of the age. It had that magical *Toy Story* feel in which they were incorporating the rest of their toys into their play with the castle, but it lacked that staying power. Soon, they were off to go play with something else.

It is not that they lacked interest in the castle and knights, but to really enjoy their new toys they needed more information.

Far from being boring, learning about things makes work and play far more interesting and enjoyable. When we read a book the following week on how to lay siege to a castle and our first book about a knight, they could not stop playing with the new toy castle. It is amazing how even a detailed and somewhat complex book can capture their attention when curiosity is piqued.

Learning and play go hand in hand. Books with engaging narratives are powerful. This chivalry challenge hinges on the use of great books to spark the imagination and open up conversations that will lead to the embodiment of the knightly ideals in everyday life.

Learning about chivalry reminds us of the importance of narrative and the role it plays in our lives. Narrative is a powerful tool used by cultures all over the world and across the expanse of time. It is the main mode for passing down history, drawing one into a community identity, teaching important lessons, and inculcating values. Narrative teaches us about the past and inspires us to act both now and in the future. Jesus used parables to teach. Charlemagne instructed Einhard to record the story of his reign. Alfred the Great had the history of the British Isles recorded. And early American history used to be a bedrock of what was taught in schools in the United States. Why? Because stories are powerful, and knowing our history instills a sense of pride in our roots and a desire to continue those ideals on which a civilization was founded.

Why do we want to introduce our boys to the grand stories of knights? Not so they can engage in bloody battles and return to feudalism. Instead, we want to inspire them to embody the ideals of chivalry, to encourage them that evil can and should be fought and to help them overcome their own weaknesses and selflessly display courage in helping others.

Stories from this period often slip into the realm of fairy tale. But fairy tales are not a waste of time. They help shape the moral imagination. They are of infinite importance in the lives of our children because, as G. K. Chesterton reminds us, "Fairy tales do not tell children the dragons exist. Children already know that dragons exist. Fairy tales tell children the dragons can be killed." There is evil in the world. There is evil lurking in the hearts of humankind. Children know this. What they need are reminders that these dragons can and ought to be defeated.

Your boys will find friends and mentors as they immerse themselves in the tales of kings such as Arthur, Charlemagne, and Alfred the Great and the stories of knights such as Lancelot, Gawain, William Marshal, Saint George, and Sir Gareth. These stories will prepare them for the training they are about to undertake.

✣ Practice Makes Progress

The more you sweat in practice,
the less you bleed in battle.

What we practice determines who we become. The formation of habits is a function of human nature. The key is to focus on developing good habits that will serve our children (and ourselves) for the rest of their lives, because the default is the unconscious formation of bad habits. Our boys will not become chivalrous overnight. We must remember that practice makes progress.

Learning about the past does indeed help us as we look toward the future. Although we are thankful we do not live within the feudal system and our future is not predetermined based on our family lineage, there is a need for chivalry now more than ever. Just like the knights of old, our kids can influence their community, and some will rise to positions of leadership in our world. We need to start training them now to be ready to take the reins of leadership—to live with integrity, to think outside of themselves, and to value the people around them. We need boys who will use their strength for the protection of others rather than to prey on others. With power and strength comes great responsibility. Let us give them a vision for what that could look like today, by embarking on an adventure into the past.

Are you ready to issue them the challenge? Are you

ready to take up this challenge yourself? You will both come away forever changed.

Here is how it works.

Collect your books. The best way to inspire the imagination and develop character comes from reading great books. In the appendix, you will find an extensive book list, ranging from fantastic picture books to chapter books for more in-depth read-aloud time or for your independent reader. These are the best of the best. Many should be available at your local library. Do not skip this step! Make it a part of your bedtime ritual or set aside some time each day to read with your child.

Do not settle for providing your kids with only fiction. Boys can be strongly drawn to nonfiction too. Finding a book that talks about knights in general or a book about medieval armor and then giving them the time to pore over it goes a long way toward fueling the imagination. Sadly, there are a growing number of books that make a mockery of knighthood. You will want to take care to avoid those.

Gather your weapons. I know, I know. Weapons are not in vogue in many circles anymore. But bear with me. We cannot inspire boys in the character side of things while denying them the opportunity to engage in imaginary warfare. I will be sharing all kinds of ideas for their physical training in the next chapter, including etiquette for (faux) battle. They need to understand that like the knights in training of centuries past, there are rules and guidelines not only for a page and squire but also for a grown-up knight as well.

Post the knight's Code of Chivalry. Print a Code of Chivalry poster and post it somewhere in your home (see p. ix). Make the announcement that knight training is to commence. Build excitement by showing them some of the books you selected, present them with a sword and shield, and then talk to them about chivalry. They need to understand this code typified the brave knights of old and that they too can embody the spirit of a knight here and now. Talk about each aspect of the code and ask them to explain what they think it means to model it in their lives. Let them know that you will be on the lookout for chivalric feats.

Track their progress. Young children between the ages of three and seven may benefit from having a visual way to chart their progress. Print and use the chart (see appendix), and when you spot your young pages living out an aspect from the code, award them a star. This can help you both see areas where they are really growing and maybe other areas where you might want to focus more attention. A chart like this is to be a temporary tool to help establish awareness and practice. The focus however should remain on becoming a knight rather than merely earning a star.

Celebrate their new identity. Although this training in chivalry will continue for the duration of your boys' childhood, set an end point for your initial foray into the world of chivalry and knight training. Celebrate by having a dubbing ceremony. Read about a knight's dubbing ceremony and decide which elements you want to include in your own.

✦ Things to Remember

Start with the big picture. Chapters six through fifteen will each outline one aspect of the code, detailing the importance of that portion historically during the times of knights as well as why it is relevant and important in today's age. Introduce the entire code at once and briefly explain each part, but then allow time to let your child focus on one aspect at a time. It is imperative to be on the lookout for examples of that aspect in action in your community and charge your boys to look for ways to embody such acts in their own lives.

Be patient and personalize training. Your young pages will not become knights overnight. Just like the boys from bygone eras, our sons need us to patiently persevere with their training. It takes time. Wise adults will challenge, but not overload their young charge. The ideas contained in this book are designed to equip you with resources and inspiration for helping your boys work on each aspect of the code. You get to pick and choose how much from each section you will do at a given time, knowing that you will continue to circle back to the Code of Chivalry for the entirety of your boys' childhood. Remember, *practice makes progress*!

Enjoy the journey. It is important to remember that by embracing the *physical aspects* of knight training we help our boys exercise the body as well as feed the imagination. By embracing the *character aspects*, we engage the soul and thus equip our children to change the world.

✦ CHAPTER 5

Physical Training
for the Quest

IT WAS A BEAUTIFUL FALL DAY, and I was back east visiting my grandparents. My oldest son was two and had already made several trips back to see them, but this was my grandparents' first time getting to meet my little two-month-old son. The boys had just woken up from naps, and I decided to take them out for a stroll before dinner. My oldest bounced into the kitchen where his doting great-grandmother was filling his sippy cup with water. I could hear them counting out ice cubes as I strapped on the baby and then ran upstairs to grab something from our room.

Coming downstairs, I found him standing next to my grandfather's chair, transfixed. He held his sippy cup in one hand and his beloved powder blue teddy cradled in the other, eyes glued to the television. As I came around the corner, I noticed that my grandfather was watching an old World War I movie. The scene that mesmerized my two-year-old son showed men firing from a foxhole and the enemy jumping into the air, falling over dead bodies—all fairly innocuous by today's movie standards. But my little guy was only two, so I scooped him up and cheerfully announced that we were off to adventure outside.

I plopped him down in a pile of leaves and turned to say something to my grandmother before setting off. Her glance behind me and subsequent smile filled me with panic. What now?

My son had transformed his powder blue teddy bear into a machine gun and was making loud rapid-fire noises as teddy's leg shot out at some imaginary enemy.

This experience left me stunned. Like many peace-loving mamas, I had sort of planned not to give my kids toy guns or maybe just have very clear rules that guns were to be used only for hunting food. I hadn't decided yet . . . But two minutes of a movie had just undone all of that. He was now all about guns, whether I provided him with them or not.

Many of us have experienced this in some form or another. There is the boy who nibbled his pb&j sandwich into the shape of a gun and was sent home from school, or the bananas that are always, always turned into guns. If not a gun, boys convert a broom or hockey stick into a rifle or that twig they found lying along the path into a swashbuckling sword. In our home, toilet paper rolls are converted into wrist guards or cut into sword sheaths. Boys live, eat, and breathe weapons.

In this chapter, I address the physical component of knight training. We start by fueling the imagination through books, boredom, as well as space and time to play. Then we give our boys the rules of engagement, the etiquette, for how to fight their battles in an honorable way. Next, I cover the many ways they can battle, from swords and jousting to archery and wrestling. Finally, I describe how physical training includes practical life skills off the battle field.

✝ Battle Wired

Honor the Imagination

Boys are hardwired to seek out the adventure of battle. We should not squash this innate drive; rather, we should cele-brate it! Boys want to be the hero, to perform heroic feats, and to come to the rescue. No modern-day knight training can be complete without physical training. This training produces the double effect of igniting the imagination and using movement to solidify hopes, dreams, and aspirations into memory, into the very fiber of who he is becoming. The imagination is powerful. If you want to effect change, capti-vate the imagination. Do you want to keep that imagination lit? Get his whole body physically involved with the process. This is critical if we want our children to embrace the spirit and heart of a knight.

As parents, grandparents, and teachers we must respect this need to imagine and this obsession to engage in battles because fighting imaginary battles prepares boys for the real ones. Becoming battle ready is a mind-set, and we want our children prepared to discover what they believe and then own it—to be willing to stand up for all that is true, honorable, and right. These battle preparations prepare the heart and mind just as much as they do the body. They promote focus and discipline.

We can honor a child's imagination by delighting in watching it at work and seeking opportunities for our children to cultivate the magic and wonder of the imagination in everyday life. This will help them not only in their quest of becoming knights but will serve them well in all their pursuits as they grow up and move into adulthood. Pretend play during childhood is no trivial pursuit. It is vital to children's health and development emotionally, socially, intellectually, and physically. This is the place where they work out their problems, dream of the future, and problem solve. In an age where everyone seems to be distracted, engaging the imagination packs an extra punch by drawing the child completely into what he is doing. It is a masterful way to effortlessly train the attention. A child may read about or hear something, but it is in the physical action of play where he cements it into long-term, meaningful memory.

Imagination can be both the *hook* and the *fuel* that feeds the learning cycle. I vividly remember the year I read *The Lion, the Witch and the Wardrobe* to my kids for the very first time. It was a magical experience. It took us a couple of chapters to get going, but then they were hooked. Eyes sparkled, attention riveted on the unfolding story. I could tell that in their minds they were in the land of Narnia. Bodies tensed and hands gripped imaginary weapons during the battle scenes. Eyes glistened a bit when Aslan was killed.

A few weeks later on a crisp Thanksgiving afternoon, my two younger sons came bounding up to me as I joined them in my in-laws' backyard. Eyes shining bright, they each grabbed a hand and pulled me forward.

"Pretend, Mom. Just pretend, OK?" they said as they revealed *the* lamppost. It was no ordinary lamppost. Forgotten was the fact that their grandpa collects them. No, this was *the* lamppost from Narnia. And just like that we stepped out of the wardrobe and into that magical realm.

Before me were King Peter and King Edmond, stick swords in hand, beckoning me to join them.

In those woods, I answered only to the name of Susan. I had a bow (yes, that curved stick I was holding), and I knew how to use it. But those "brothers" of mine were quite protective. Edmond insisted on taking up the rear to keep me safe between the two of them as we traipsed through the bit of woods we had there.

The boys battled. We hunted for food and roasted wild turkeys. A debate erupted about which would make a better bone broth—deer bones or turkey bones. I smiled, thrilled to watch them work out some of the nutrition lessons we have learned. We scaled the old crumbling walls of Cair Paravel while the boys discussed battle plans; we went in search of beavers. Grandpa found us, informing us about a real beaver family that lives in the creek by his woods. He showed us the tree they felled. Eyes grew wide as our imaginative play hit a stroke of concurrent reality.

The imagination is a powerful tool. Once lit, it propels kids painlessly into worlds of creative output. It kindles the formation of their own stories and is a delight to behold. *I am reminded again to guard their time—this precious time to play, to pretend, to become. I am inspired afresh to find great books on which their vivid imaginations can feast.* I am thankful that they grab my hand and pull me into the magic and wonder of a child's imagination.

I do not often enter their imaginary worlds, but when I do, it is a fresh reminder of the power vested in the imagination. When we feed our kids great ideas through powerful stories, the imagination is unleashed to do what it does best. And that is what we want to take advantage of in this current quest of training knights.

We want to feed them great ideas, inspire them with the tales of knights of old and then unleash their imagination. This means guarding their schedules so they have time to read, time to play—free from constantly taking them from activity to activity or allowing them to fill every spare waking moment in front of some kind of screen. We need to prioritize time to enter other realms. For some of us, this will mean having to set better boundaries with our children's devices and allowing them some room for boredom.

As odd as it may sound, boredom is the constant companion of curiosity, creativity, and the imagination. In the frenetic pace of our culture we must be intentional to cultivate this kind of time. In my home growing up, any child who whined about boredom was immediately assigned a new chore. We learned quick to find creative ways to occupy our time. If you want to help your children's imaginations grow, give them time for boredom. Provide great books, maybe a few costumes or props, and then turn them loose!

World-renowned child developmental psychologist David Elkind contends that "children's play—their inborn disposition for learning, curiosity, imagination, and fantasy—is being silenced in the high-tech, commercialized work we have created." He also notes that "over the past several decades, children have lost twelve hours of free time a week, including eight hours of unstructured play and outdoor activities."[1]

But this does not have to be the reality for your family. Time for imaginative play, for reading great books, and for character development (all key elements for this kind of knight training) can happen when we choose to buck trends in our culture. You have the power to set the climate and culture for your own family. How can you give your kids the gift of time to cultivate their imaginations and all the benefits that go along with this?

Protect your schedule. Time is the magic ingredient. Imaginative play takes time. Slowing down long enough to enjoy and immerse ourselves in a good book takes time. And finally, training takes time.

Limit screen time. Research over and over again has pointed to the ill effects screen time (TV, phones, tab-

---

1. David Elkind, *The Power of Play* (Cambridge: De Capo Press, 2007), p. ix.

lets) has on children, from childhood obesity and irregular sleep patterns to social and/or behavioral issues. We need to take stock of our children's media habits and set parameters so there are chunks of time in their day that are reliably screen free and reserved for imaginative play and reading.

Boot them outdoors. Kids, boys especially, have a lot of energy. We need to take a tip from our parent's playbooks and boot our kids outdoors. Encourage them to play, explore, and enjoy the fresh air. Instead of parking them in front of a screen while you prepare dinner, send them outside.

Recognizing that boys are battle wired and valuing the role of imaginative play in the developmental process helps us embrace these out-of-the-box learning opportunities. We must let them engage in play battles, but we can set up some caveats.

✝ Rules of Engagement

It is wise to establish rules of engagement for your knight in training—both for your sanity and his safety.

A knight understands the value of ingenuity during battle but carefully balances this with the importance of always fighting fair. By all means think creatively, but fight with honor and integrity.

As the ruling king or queen of your home it is important to communicate to your up-and-coming page or squire the rules of battle. Set clear boundaries for fighting fair as well as consequences for breach of etiquette. In our home, weapons are confiscated and couch time or early bedtimes are meted out for offending young knights when protocol is breached.

Here are a few of our rules. We adjust them depending on context and the ages of our kids.

- Keep above the belt and below the neck—a true knight in training never, ever aims at the face, or takes that cheap shot below the belt.
- Weapon on weapon should be the focus of sparring. (Remember, this is just practice.)
- Never attack an unarmed man.
- Never attack from behind. We do not stab people in the back. That is what cowards do. Challenge your opponent to a duel, but do not resort to cowardly tactics.
- Arrows or other projectile kinds of weapons are aimed at targets, not people.

✢ Arm Them for Battle Play

Swords

Playing with swords is not going to turn your child into some sort of violent psychopath, especially when paired with the rest of the knight training. Your young squire will learn to treat his weapon with respect; he will use it in the context of the rules of engagement as he seeks the honorable road of "fighting fair." This can and should be a regular part of a boy's rough and tumble play.

Buy them or make them! Of course, any old stick will do. But if you want to give your children the flexibility of bringing them indoors or want to blunt the pain factor if they get hit, I recommend foam. When my kids were really young, I used to snag foam swords from the dollar bin at various stores. As the kids got older, we liked to use PVC pipes to fashion swords, covering them with foam pipe covers and duct-taping them down. These can still hurt, but they lend the feel of a more mature sword. Boys of all ages love them.

Most boys need no instruction to get going (aside from the rules for fair engagement, which need to be repeated again and again and again . . .) For younger boys, it is advisable to focus on sword-on-sword practice. Depending on age and context, you might even want to prohibit physical contact. But if you are looking to mix up your sword battles, here are a few ideas:

◆ Play the classic game Swords and Bucklers, which all pages would play to hone their fledgling sword skills. It is a game still popular today with sword enthusiasts of all ages. The point of the game is to use your sword to deal blows and your buckler, a mini shield, to deflect blows. You can simply play for the pure joy of sparring or keep score and declare a winner. To keep score, a person gets 1 point for a touch to the arms and 5 points for a touch to the torso. The first to reach 10 points wins that match. A hit above the shoulders or below the belt is an automatic victory for the other person. Pot lids stand in beautifully for bucklers.

✦ Find a hill and practice either body tag or simply sword on sword battles, giving one child the hill. This will be an excellent opportunity to discuss the benefit of the high ground and having situational awareness. How could you use a hill to your advantage? Can your child think of any other environmental or physical situations to use to their advantage (sun in the eyes, trees, a wall, etc.)?

Jousting

Jousting tournaments are probably one of the most iconic visuals of the Middle Ages. Tournaments were a fun way for knights to demonstrate their prowess and excellent battle skills. Setting up a jousting tournament is a must for your budding young squires.

Here is how to whip up some super-quick jousting sticks. You will need pool noodles and electrician's tape. Wrap the electrician's tape in a spiral formation around the pool noodle for a quick transformation to get you going with some jousting games. Grab your trusty steed (stick horse or bike), helmet, and jousting stick for some medieval fun.

Aim straight. Head out to the sidewalk. One person holds up a large hoop or box to give your knights in training something to aim for. Show them how to grip the pool noodle between their upper arm and torso, aim forward and let them spur (or spin) their mighty steeds forward. Up the challenge by suspending a pool ring and seeing if they can hook it on the next turn.

Joust challenge. Set up empty cans along a route. Have your knight mount his steed (bike or stick horse) and see how many cans he can topple on his run through the course. The bike adds an extra challenge, and if your kids want even more, you could time them to determine who can do it the fastest.

Archery

Any boy who has seen Errol Flynn's *Robin Hood* movie will be determined never to be without a sword and bow and arrows. One of my boys even converted a little plastic golf club canister into his quiver so he could easily tote his bow and arrows wherever he went.

Suction-cup bow and arrow set. For young kids, I highly recommend suction-cup arrow sets. They do not last forever, but long after our arrows snapped, the kids would still play with the bow and were forever creative in coming up with new ways to make their own arrows or simply use their imaginations. Use a dry erase marker on a large window or glassed door to create a target and take aim. If they are having a hard time getting their arrows to stick an alternative is to shoot them through a plastic hoop. During our intense knight-training periods, we would pull out the bow and arrows every single day.

For older children, consider a youth bow and arrow set. The arrows in a youth archery set usually come with blunted practice tips. Purchase a hay bale from a feed store and attach a target to begin the challenge. Shooting an arrow properly takes a surprising amount of focus and is a great activity to hone attention and body control. Your kids will have a whole new respect for the knights of old who could shoot with precision and accuracy at the snap of a finger.

Climbing Skills

While a knight's primary place was on his horse, he needed to know how to climb as well. As such, pages and squires spent time climbing—trees, walls, or any other obstacle. Take your budding knight out to a baseball diamond and let him practice climbing the chain-link fence. Find other structures in your area where he can continue to develop these skills.

Wrestling

Wrestling is another activity that took up a good deal of a boy's time. Knights were warriors and, as such, had to be prepared for any scenario, including times when he might be unseated or separated from his sword. Wrestling develops the vestibular system, which integrates the body's senses, enabling balance and coordinated movement. It also strengthens a boy's ability to problem solve. Both are essential for a knight's survival. Wrestling helped him combine strength with agility and is just plain fun. Here are a few medieval-themed ideas:

Cross the bridge. Set aside an area to be your "bridge." The object of this game is to be the first knight to make it across without getting pinned down by the giant. In this game a young knightling is given the quest to storm the castle and rescue the royal family. The giant, aka Dad, guards the bridge and the weaponless knights must figure a way to get across without being captured by the giant who is bent on tickling young knights to death.

Finger jousting. This fast-paced wrestling game is best played with two people of similar height. The point of the game is to touch your pointer finger to the arms, legs, or torso of your opponent. You get 1 point for a leg or arm contact and 2 points for a torso touch. The first person to get 10 points wins the match. Lock hands in a wrestling stance with pointer fingers sticking out (your joust). The other arm must be held behind your back and while you can move your feet to position yourself, you cannot use your legs or opposite arm in this joust.

Stand your ground challenge. Two kids face each other with feet apart at hip width and about 12 inches from their opponent's feet, palms touching at shoulder height. Each tries to push the other's hands until one is forced to take a step. Palms must remain at shoulder height. Victory goes to the opponent who can hold his ground. Play best two out of three.

Squire's Work

While the ultimate goal was to become a mighty warrior, a page and squire spent most of their time on other duties that, in a roundabout way, prepared them for their chosen vocation in addition to helping the castle run smoothly. A well-disciplined boy, able to pay attention to detail and work hard, had the makings to become a mighty knight. He also learned about how the foundation of chivalry affected life outside of the battlefield.

No knight's training could be complete without developing and practicing these everyday skills and your knights in the making can benefit too.

Learn the art of setting the table and bringing food. A page helped during mealtimes by bringing in food and dishes and helping clear everything away—every day and at every meal. If your young page isn't already doing this, institute this as part of his castle training and newly assigned duties. A well-run castle means everyone has a role to play and a way to contribute. In addition, plan a fancier dinner to teach him proper etiquette: how to set a fancy dinner table with the salad fork, dinner fork, dessert spoon, and so on and how each utensil is used during a meal. Teach your page how to place food platters responsibly on the table and how to pass food (pick either clockwise or counterclockwise and be consistent).

Learn how to sharpen knives. Keeping the daggers, knives, and swords sharp was an important job. If you have a knife sharpener in your home, teach your young page how to use it. If you are anything like me, you may not even know how to do this yourself. YouTube is a great resource for knife sharpening tutorials (see, for example, youtu.be/oIz8QNVb4P8). As always when handling sharp tools, be very careful.

Learn to care for your king or queen's steed. A page learned general horse care during their younger years and took on full responsibility for the particular care of their knight's horses, armor, and tack in his teen years. Horses are no longer our primary mode of transportation, so a modern-day knight in training learns the art and discipline of cleaning the car—inside and out.

Learn to care for your own trusty steed. Bicycle care is another area for your knight in training to work on. Encourage your squire to

> Always put his steed in the stables.
> Learn how to pump up bike tires.
> Periodically make sure his bike gets a good wipe down.
> Clean the chain with a degreaser, old toothbrush, and rag a couple of times a year. Then he should relube the chain to maintain peak performance and durability.

Learn how to shine silver. Pages and squires were responsible for shining up the armor and keeping it in tip-top shape. If you have any silver, put your boys to work shining it up. This might necessitate a trip to Grandma's. Shine on, shine off, young squires.

Tidy up your knight's abode. A knight in training was responsible for keeping the living quarters tidy. While you won't require him to clean up your room, you can certainly use that as a threat when he complains about tidying up his own room or helping with the general living areas.

✛ CHAPTER 6

The Code: Love God

✛ *Love the Lord Your God with Your Heart, Soul, Mind, and Strength*

A knight knows that his love for God is the fuel that motivates everything else he does. He seeks to know God, to honor God, and to give loyalty first and foremost to God. He pledges to love God not just in word but also in deed by serving him with his whole heart, soul, mind, and strength.

VIKING KING GUTHRUM and his men launched a surprise attack on a cold night in A.D. 878, knowing that King Alfred and all his Saxon men were busy celebrating Twelfth Night—the grand climax of the Christmas season at that time. Guthrum's decisive victory was nearly everything he had hoped it would be: The Saxon stronghold was decimated, and the people scattered. Providentially, Alfred managed to escape alive.

For years, the Vikings had swept through England, raiding, pillaging, and leaving destruction in their wake. Repeatedly, the Saxons had paid ransom to buy a truce, only to have the Viking forces go back on their word.

Nestled deep in the swamplands of Athelney, King Alfred made plans to win his kingdom back from this lawless horde.

After Alfred laid siege to the Viking stronghold at Chippenham and successfully prevailed, Guthrum himself came out, hoping against hope that he could offer his life in exchange for the release of his starving men. What happened next blew him away.

Despite a history of broken treaties, Alfred extended mercy not only to his men, but also to Guthrum himself.

> *"What mean you by this? What is your plan here?"*
>   *stammered Guthrum.*
> *"I serve a God who is merciful, so how can I not extend*
>   *mercy to you?" Alfred replied.*
> *"You know what we do to kings we capture? I would have*
>   *gladly torn you limb from limb."*
> *Alfred nods.*
> *"I must know more of this God of yours."*[1]

And so they met to discuss the treaty. Alfred the Great, as he would come to be known, entertained Guthrum and his

---

1. This meeting between Guthrum and Alfred was chronicled by Alfred's biographer, Asser. This is how I imagine the conversation went.

men for twelve days, whereupon Guthrum and thirty of his bravest men converted to Christianity.

Enemies were transformed into allies. It is difficult to say whether Guthrum's conversion was genuine, but we do know that he maintained peace and was content with the land that Alfred graciously extended to him.

Thanks to Alfred's biographers, the world would continue to hear of his worthy deeds as he set about creating peace and order in his realm through just laws and educational reform. Stories of his valor and his faith, which motivated his actions, continue to inspire people throughout the Middle Ages and today.

FOR THE KNIGHTS OF OLD, love for God provided the motivation and moral framework on which their work took shape and force. Knights believed they owed allegiance first to the kingdom of God and to society as a whole, rather than merely to their earthly lord. It gave them purpose beyond just the temporal. In other words, their love for God provided the *why* for defending the defenseless, helping the helpless, and loving the unloved.

✝ Knights and the Faith

The knights of old were repeatedly called to recognize that life is a gift, and they were to live for something more than themselves. This was not a one-time commitment, but rather a day-in, day-out recentering of their lives. Our knights in training flourish when this foundation is in place because it motivates them to live consistent, compassionate lives of service to both God and the people they encounter each day. Reading about the knights of old provides the context for discussing how a knight's faith informed his actions and opens a door to talk about what it can mean when we do the same through our own faith traditions. These stories give a glimpse into how they chose to honor God in the way they lived their lives rather than simply following their passions. This allows us to then help our young squires see the big picture perspective so that they too can pursue what is right and good, regardless of how they might feel at any given moment.

While these stories are not primarily about faith, we see bits and pieces of this woven through all of them, sometimes more obvious than others.

Saint George

Tales of Saint George have mesmerized people of many cultures. England and several other countries claim him as their patron saint. He is also considered the patron saint of chivalry, soldiers, and at one point even the Boy Scouts. Historically, the George who inspired the legend was a third-century Roman soldier serving under Emperor Diocletian who was martyred because he refused to recant his Christian faith.

His life sparked many legends depicted in fanciful retellings and glorious works of art. I have a thing for beautifully illustrated picture books that weave fantastic tales, so it came as no surprise when my parents gave me one of my childhood favorites shortly after I graduated from college. Margaret Hodges's classic *St. George and the Dragon* is the very first medieval tale I read to my kids.

In this recounting, George, the Red Cross Knight, takes up the seemingly impossible task of freeing a terrorized people from a fierce dragon. As George journeys to the dragon, he meets a hermit who takes him up to a hilltop where he catches a glimpse of the Celestial City, representing heaven. He declares his desire to go to this perfect place at once. Who wouldn't? But the old hermit responds, "That High City that you see is in another world. Before you climb the path to it and hang your shield on its wall, go down into the valley and fight the dragon that you were sent to fight." And this sets the tone for the rest of the book, which vividly recounts the fierce battle he faced. The striking illustrations and beautiful words captivate us each and every time we read it. My boys tense, totally enthralled with the drama of this epic battle, longing with every fiber of their being to embark on a similar quest.

This book highlights beautiful and inspiring religious imagery of that time. The dragon represents Satan and the spiritual aspects of this battle. The Red Cross Knight courageously fought the dragon for a period of three days, mirroring the three days between the crucifixion of Jesus and his resurrection. The importance of divine purpose and the power of prayer and perseverance are delicately interwoven throughout.

The quickest way to make a great book a great bore is to make everything a lesson. Kids don't respond to lectures well, but they do enjoy conversations. Sometimes we do nothing but read the story and let the words and illustrations speak for themselves. Other times, I'll pose a question such as asking if they know how many days it took George to defeat the dragon, and then ponder out loud if that number might be significant. Other times we might linger over a page and study the pictures. Someone will notice the Lady Una praying in the background. The key here is to look for opportunities for natural conversations and then go with the flow.

Books like this provide fertile ground for planting seeds of conversation about the interplay between belief and action, faith and fear, between now and forever. These tales about Saint George developed over time to motivate aspiring and existing knights to recognize their holy calling and take action to fight against evil and injustice here on this earth. Let these books make the clarion call to our boys as well.

Lancelot

The legends surrounding Lancelot are another example of subtle faith stories. In the picture book *Young Lancelot*, we learn that he is indeed strong and valiant. We are swept up in his adventures as he sets out to prove himself the worthiest knight of all. We cheer at his ingenuity and bravery and find ourselves holding our breath when he is at the Chapel

Perilous fighting an impossible foe—a foe he can defeat only when he puts the needs of others before his own.

This strong connection between faith and fealty, between God and knights, has a long history. According to historians, Saint Augustine taught "the happiness of the ruler lay in just rule, in the fear of God, and in the love of the heavenly kingdom."[2] His writings in the early fifth century set the foundation for the ideal of what a medieval European king should be like, which filtered down to the mightiest warriors.

The warrior king Charlemagne took this to heart as he sought to unite the splintered factions of Europe in the chaos unleashed after the fall of the Roman Empire.

For all his imperfections, and he had many, Charlemagne is responsible for setting the tone of how the Christian faith and ethic would come to undergird much of medieval society for the next millennium. For him, the role of the ideal ruler and the ideal warrior could be summarized thus: Defend the oppressed, take up the cause of the fatherless, and plead the case of the widow. These are all ideas he drew from the Bible.

He issued the call for the knights of his time to pursue passionate dedication of their lives in service not only to an earthly king but also to *The King* who transcends time and geography.

---

2. Beatrice Lees, *Alfred the Great: The Truth Teller* (Berlin: Andesite Press, 2015), p. 15.

Roland

We see the interplay between faith and service in *The Song of Roland*, which lays the foundation for the ideas behind chivalry. Roland's faith reflects the deep-seated belief in Charlemagne's court. This is a deeply personal faith, through which Roland and others cry out directly to God for help in their time of peril, for salvation when death draws nigh, and for righting of wrongs. As Roland breathes his last, the poem reads:

> *Now Roland feels death press upon him hard;*
> *It is creeping down from his head to his heart.*
> *And many things begin to call to mind:*
> *All the broad lands he conquered in his time,*
> *And fairest France, and the men of his line,*
> *And Charles his lord, who bred him from a child;*
> *He cannot help but weep for them and sigh.*
> *Yet of himself he is mindful betimes;*
> *He beats his breast and on God's mercy cries:*
> *"Father most true, in whom there is no lie,*
> *Who didst from death St Lazarus make to rise,*
> *And bring out Daniel safe from the lions' might,*
> *Save though my soul from danger and despite*
> *Of all the sins I did in all my life."*
> *His right-hand glove he tendered unto Christ,*
> *And from his hand Gabriel accepts the sign.*
> *Strait away his head upon his arm declines;*
> *With folded hands he makes an end and dies.*

Alfred

King Alfred the Great ruled just a few decades after Charlemagne and set a similar tone in England. Instead of trying to expand his territory and create an empire, however, Alfred's purpose during his wartime endeavors was to protect his land and people. As a warrior king, he set the tone for his men in valiantly defending the weak and winning friends who had previously been counted enemies. His reign was pivotal not only for the future of England but for developing the course of the knightly class and the nobility in the centuries ahead. He sought to establish a principled foundation based directly on the laws of God, as revealed in the Bible, that might abolish the blood feuds that were rampant between the warring chieftains and thus establish law and order. He credits his faith with pulling him through all that he endured—a faith that took root during his boyhood.

Geoffroi de Charny

By the time of Geoffroi de Charny, in the fourteenth century, love for God and knightly service were inextricably linked. His book on chivalry was a call for knights to return to the ideal and references to God were liberally strewn throughout. He was as manly as they came, and devotion to God was a part of that. As for service to God, he viewed the knightly call as important as a vocation in the church. De Charny contended that you cannot possess true knighthood apart from a foundation of love for God.

✢ What Is Love of God?

Taken together, all these stories illustrate the importance of loving God. But what does it mean to love God with your heart, soul, mind, and strength? To love God (or anyone for that matter), we must know him—know his character. Theologians have spilled vats of ink describing God's nature. Boys tend to be especially interested in the attributes that emphasize God's power, intelligence, and size juxtaposed with his interest and compassion for them individually. In other words, God as the ultimate football coach who is the smartest, mightiest man on the team who expects great things from his men but also knows them each individually and cares about them.

It has been said that when a man walks into a room, he sizes up each of the men present and asks himself, "Could I take him?" His respect stems from that. Well, God, for a boy, is the man in the room who no one can take but who is also completely on his side. From this love for God stems respect, loyalty, and honor for him with powerful, practical results.

One of the most important ramifications of knightly "love of God" was the recognition of the Imago Dei. This Latin term for "image of God" is a central idea that permeated much of Christian thought through the Middle Ages and continues to influence people today, especially in the area of human rights theory. When someone loves and honors God, they recognize that all people have worth because they are created in the image of God. Their intrinsic worth does not spring from their productiveness, their beauty, or what they contribute to society, but simply *because they are human.*

While simple in theory, humanity often surprisingly gets the Imago Dei wrong. Throughout history we have excused bigotry, prejudice, abuse, and even extermination in the name of perceived superiority or because we elevate convenience and productivity above human worth. When humanity gets it right, however, the world is literally changed. Recognizing others as equally human makes differences fade; it promotes an idea of innate dignity for each human being. It is this dignity and respect for people that changes the way society functioned and how people treated one another. As Desmond Tutu wrote, "An authentic Christian spirituality is utterly subversive to any system that would treat a man or woman as anything less than a child of God. . . . Every praying Christian, every person who has an encounter with God, must have a passionate concern for his or her brother and sister, his or her neighbor."

The rest of the chivalric code hinges on the Imago Dei. As you honor God, you will honor, care for, and defend those created in his image—other people. You will treat them the way you would want to be treated.

✠ Why Does Belief in God Matter?

There is a litany of other practical reasons to acknowledge a God greater than yourself, and they apply as much for the knights of old as they do for the boys of today. From the love of God, they find a reason to conquer selfishness, live with virtue, discover their purpose, and embrace hope.

Acknowledging God provides security because we recognize that immutable truth and ultimate authority is not found in mere humans. Without this foundation, might makes right and whoever happens to be in charge gets to make the rules. The idea of this kind of relative truth does not sit well with most people, which is why we seek to overthrow tyrannical rulers even if it means we personally do not get to rule. It was this awareness that drove the top knights in thirteenth-century England to force the selfish King John (the little brother to Richard the Lionheart) to sign the Magna Carta, which established that there were principles and laws, under God, that superseded even the king.

In addition to providing the foundation for how and why we live, belief in God also gives us:

A Reason to Live Outside of Oneself

Charlemagne realized that a mighty warrior who recognized no higher authority would be a mercenary—hiring himself out to the highest bidder or preying on whoever came across his path. When selfishness reigns supreme there is no one to trust because everyone is out to seek his own good. Peace is an impossibility on every level. Anarchy and chaos become the unrelenting reality.

It does not take long into the parenting journey to discover a universal truth about people everywhere. It is a truth on full and sometimes embarrassing display among our toddlers and preschoolers, manifesting itself best in the form of tantrums. That truth is that people are selfish. If you are the honest sort, you will recognize these temptations and tendencies in yourself as well. With the rise of rampant narcissism and the culture of self-promotion that social media affords, it is perhaps more obvious now than ever before. Learning to honor God gives you a reason to subdue your inherent selfishness and focus on the needs of others.

A Reason to Live with Virtue

Love for God recognizes that there is something, some*one* who is transcendent. There is definite right and wrong, and it is love and loyalty to God that motivates people to act in ways that benefit others, that build culture, and that cultivate community. Loyalty to God fuels loyalty to leaders, it fuels fighting against injustice, and it fuels caring for the weak. Without God, who decides what is unjust or wrong after all? It would merely be at the whim of whoever is in charge and will rapidly change when some other selfish person gains control.

When we recognize universal principles and acknowledge the one who put them in place, it gives us a reason to live with virtue. Behavior is birthed out of belief.

It was this acknowledgment of God that is the foundational principle for the entire Code of Chivalry that developed during the medieval period. For the knight, this provided the overarching principle, the *why* for what he did—love and honor for God and subsequently love for others.

A Reason to Live with Purpose

There is an innate drive in most of us to find purpose in what we do. We all want to know that our lives matter, that there is a reason for us being here at this time, in this place. Acknowledging God and seeking to honor him also gives us a reason to live with purpose because we realize God has a role for each person in this life.

Although we are told to follow our dreams to find purpose, the reality is that living only for our dreams does not ultimately satisfy. Even the most amazing feats can ring hollow as Tom Brady Jr., quarterback for the New England Patriots, revealed in a *60 Minutes* interview: "Why do I have three Super Bowl rings and still think there is something greater out there for me? . . . I reached my goal, my dream, my life. It's got to be more than this."

Michael Phelps, one of the most decorated athletes in Olympic history, also felt adrift after his great victories of the 2012 Olympics. He revealed, "I was a train wreck. I was like a time bomb, waiting to go off. I had no self-esteem, no self-worth. There were times where I didn't want to be here. It was not good. I felt lost." His perspective radically changed after a friend recommended he read *The Purpose Driven Life*, a book that, Phelps says, "turned me into believing that there is a power greater than myself and there is a purpose for me on this planet."

Being the best at what you do does not give your life meaning and purpose. De Charny called his knights back to their ultimate purpose, he reminded them that acknowledging God and recognizing the role they play in God's plan provides lasting purpose that transcends mere physical accomplishments that even both Brady and Phelps acknowledge do not satisfy.

A Reason to Live with Hope

Love for God also allows us to live with hope. We know there is evil in the world; we see it every day on the news. As our children see in the story of Saint George, there is a battle going on between good and evil, but ultimately good can and will triumph. This knowledge gives us hope.

✢ Passing On Our Faith
_____

We live in a time when many care little for anything outside of themselves and what satisfies their own desires. Many boys are adrift without drive; they seem lost without hope. Turning to the knight's Code of Chivalry, we are reminded to inspire our boys to love and honor God. As parents, we are in a unique situation to bring our children into our own faith traditions, to have deep conversations, and to model what it means to love and honor God.

We get to show our boys that living a God-centered life provides the framework for the kind of purposeful and fulfilling life that we all crave. We have the opportunity to invite them into this grand adventure and help them understand that faith is not just a heart thing; faith in God affects every other area of our lives as well. It is a lifelong quest well worth embarking on.

✢ Throwing Down the Gauntlet

Passing on our faith does not happen by default. We need to make the conscious choice to be intentional in our interactions with our children. As the king or queen of your home, take some time to think through what this will look like for your family. Here are a few suggestions to get you going.

Engaging in bedtime prayer. The simple act of bedtime prayers can be powerful. Acknowledge God and his immutable attributes. Pray for friends and loved ones. Pray for protection. Thank God, the author of life, for your day.

Participating in mealtime prayer. Help your knight in training learn gratitude by thanking God for food.

Learning the Lord's Prayer. The Lord's Prayer has been memorized and recited for nearly two thousand years. It is both instructional and inspirational.

> *Our Father which art in heaven,*
> *Hallowed be thy name.*
> *Thy kingdom come. Thy will be done*
> *on earth, as it is in heaven.*
> *Give us this day our daily bread.*
> *And forgive us our debts,*
> *as we forgive our debtors.*
> *And lead us not into temptation,*
> *but deliver us from evil:*
> *For thine is the kingdom, and the power,*
> *and the glory, forever. Amen.*

Attending religious services. Make regular attendance at your place of worship a habit instead of a happenstance. We need God and we need others. We were meant to live in community with others; this is how we grow and how we are challenged.

Discuss with your young squire how to honor God in that place. In most Christian faiths, a gentleman takes off his hat. Within some sects of the Jewish faith men wear a yarmulke. While roughhousing is to be enjoyed in some places, a house of worship is not the place for loud voices and boisterous play. This is not the time or place to seek entertainment and distraction with an electronic device.

It is a time to be still, to listen, to receive, and to respond appropriately.

Some faith traditions call for kneeling to show submission to God. In other traditions, you lift your hands when you pray or sing. Encourage your children to do these physical aspects of devotion of your faith's traditions both in a church setting as well as in the privacy of your home.

Honoring God with your voice. Learn a religious song of your choice such as "The Doxology," "Amazing Grace," or the traditional American spiritual "He's Got the Whole World in His Hands."

Recognizing the source of your moral framework. Follow in Charlemagne's example and build the daily reading of God's words into your child's routine. Some families read a psalm every morning, other families read a chapter out of the book of Proverbs, and others do a reading from the Bible before bed. Hearts and minds are changed by what we read.

✦ CHAPTER 7

The Code: Obey

> ### ✦ *Obey Those in Authority over You*
>
> A true knight understands the value of leadership and authority. A knight of worth recognizes that to lead well, one must first learn to follow.

"WELL, let's ask the king of the home." We sat gathered around the table, sharing a family meal when the boys reminded me about a question they had asked earlier that day. As we read about the lives of knights, we learned that loyalty to God and king (or queen) were paramount and obedience during their training years was essential. I asked these young squires of mine who was the king of our castle. "Dad," came the chorus of responses. It was a lightbulb moment.

There are realms of authority everywhere, and although

we do not live in a country with a monarchy, we still see the need for order, leadership, government, and responsibility. Mom is not allowed to speed because it violates the law of the land. Boys know this, because a man in a nice shiny car with lights on top reminded them that one time . . . Dad cannot decide each day whether or not he feels like heading in to work. He is under authority and noncompliance means no job. We are all responsible to those in authority over us. For our children, that primary authority rests with us. They depend on our leadership to keep them safe, to guide them, to prepare them for the time when they will have their own realms of leadership whether that is in the home, the community, or the workplace. Our children must learn how to obey.

We live in a mixed-up world where children often sit on the throne and parents seek to carefully appease them, fearful that taking charge might alienate them. The word *obey* has become a four-letter word and parents are fed the lie that obedient children lead to mindlessly compliant adults. When parents do not embrace the call to lead, children rule the roost. This is a role they are not prepared to handle yet.

Instead of having a child-centered home, we need to shift to a family-centered one in which we recognize our role as benevolent rulers. Learning to respect our authority prepares our children to interact with other appropriate realms of authority and to one day lead within their own. We must not abdicate our role as king and queen of the home realm.

What characterizes an ideal ruler? How can this inspire and equip us in our parenting journey? The world of kings, queens, knights, and squires has much to teach us about parent–child relationships. When we think of the ideal, we imagine someone who is just and yet merciful. We think of someone who has a deep love for his people and his realm. He rules with their ultimate best interests at heart. We think of someone who is compassionate and loving, loyal (to his people), and strong. A good ruler is future focused, looking toward seeking the health and continuation of their realm. A good ruler sees the big picture and does what is best for his people, even if they balk at the discomfort of the moment.

Does this not remind you of the ideal parent? Except our children are not just the average people of a realm. The stakes are especially high because these are the people we love most.

It was a ruler's job to provide protection, order, preparation, and continuation of the kingdom. Those are duties that we share as well today. As we help our children form a habit of obedience, we are better able to carry out our role in preparing them for the future. We cannot protect them if they will not listen to us. We cannot create peace and order in their lives where chaos rules. We cannot prepare them for the future when mutual love and respect are absent.

It has been six years now since we first embarked on this chivalry challenge and internalized these concepts. Since then our appreciation has continued to grow. We realize that we are in this adventure together. They may not understand all our decisions, but there is an awareness of our purpose and their role during this phase of their lives.

When we recognize and embrace the roles we are called to play as king and queen of the home realm, it becomes easier to remember that we are training the leaders of tomorrow. Leadership begins by learning about true justice, appropriate and inappropriate realms of authority, and obedience to proper authorities.

Pages and squires learned these truths from the king and queen of the castle and then from their knight. Our children primarily learn these truths from us. A page first learned how to serve, how to follow directions, and how to obey within the context of the home realm. These skills of service and obedience were not time fillers, these chores laid the foundation for everything else in his life by developing self-control and learning the discipline of hard work.

Much of this early training took place under the direction of the women in the household. When he became a squire that training transferred to a knight, who would model and teach him the art of being a man and a warrior.

Children need this authority in their lives. They balk, as we all do, at authority. Humanity's desire is to call our own shots, to be our own man (or woman). This inherently wired propensity to defy authority is within each of us and it takes intentional training to curb that desire for self-centered living.

Psychologist and parenting expert John Rosemond explains that while we spend the first eighteen months of a child's life making him feel as if he were the center of the universe, we must spend the following eighteen years convincing him he is not.[1] Helping our children learn these lessons in the early years not only makes your life easier, but also helps train them to learn from you and other adults in their lives. A three-year-old throwing a tantrum because he did not get his way is one thing, a teenager or, worse yet, an adult throwing one is entirely different.

It is important for our knights in training to realize they are not full-fledged knights yet. They are growing and developing. They do not get to call the shots. This is their training phase. It is our job to lead and theirs to follow.

✠ Say What You Mean, Mean What You Say

Parenting is exhausting—but sometimes we make it harder than it has to be. It took someone far older and wiser than I am to help me zero in on a fatal mistake I was making early in the parenting journey. I had a habit of trying to sneak in directives in the form of questions. It would go something like this. "Hey sweetie, would you like some salad?" "I'd rather not, Mommy," came the reply. Stunned by his polite but incorrect answer to my question, I would amend my words. "I'm sorry, let me rephrase that. You will eat your salad now." It was a classic parenting mistake that is entirely all too common these days.

"Do you want to go to the store?" "Not really."

---

1. John Rosemond, *A Family of Value* (Kansas City: Andrews and McNeel, 1995).

"Would you like to go to bed?" "Nope."

Asking questions when we really mean to give a command is both ineffective and dishonest. Clear communication that is kind and firm, and matter-of-fact works best.

"You need to finish your salad before you can be excused." "It is time to go to the store now." "Bedtime."

You can still give choices within the boundaries of what they need to do. Instead of asking your children if they want oatmeal for breakfast, ask them if they want cinnamon or chocolate flavored oatmeal. Instead of "Would you like water?" ask them "Do you want your water in the red cup or the blue cup?" You get to give them some of the flexibility and control they want, but within the boundaries of what you know is best for them.

Knowing that you will say what you mean and mean what you say helps our children because they can deal with your statements at face value rather than trying to decipher whether you are offering a true choice. When clarifying communication, pause and ask yourself, "Is this a question or a command?"

✠ Moving Toward the Why

Our kids are in the middle childhood years now. It is glorious. We sleep through the night, there are no bottoms to wipe, and they can prepare their own breakfast and lunch. But in some ways it is more challenging. We have moved beyond just "obey because we say so" to needing to pass along the rationale. As they get older, we want to help them understand *why* we are making the decisions we make. They are coming into the age at which they need to start wrestling with these whys. Naturally our kids do not agree with all of our decisions. Explaining *why* we have made our decision, *why* we said no to something, or *why* they are receiving said consequence for disobedience prepares them to one day make their own decisions. Sometimes we hear ourselves echoing our own parents: "When you are a grown-up you can do things differently. But for now, as your parents, we've chosen this course for our family."

As we move into the teen years, another transition will occur. We will start the process of handing more decisions over to them as they become increasingly independent.

We want a home where respect is breathed into the fabric of everyday living, where respect guides our interactions with each other—husband to wife, parent to child, and child to child.

Good kings or queens guide their people well. They recognize that the people under their care are unique, one-of-a-kind individuals with thoughts and feelings. As such they treat them with special love and care. They provide clear communication and direction.

This kind of respect is infectious. When we recognize our children as people, made in the Imago Dei, and properly steward the job of raising them, it is easier for them to reflect respect back and extend it to others.

✠ To Lead, You Must First Learn to Follow

The warrior mentality runs deep in my family. As a new mom, I would frequently take my young sons back to visit my elderly grandparents. On one visit, my grandfather pulled me aside, asking if we could talk. With an intense look of love and determination he launched into his pep talk.

"You cannot lead unless you first learn to follow."

I must have given him a confused look because he settled back deep in thought. After reflection, he leaned forward once more.

"Heather, learning how to obey and respect authority is one of the most important skills you can help them develop." He then began to reminisce about his childhood and his years at West Point as he prepared to follow in his father's footsteps by serving in the U.S. Army.

"The plebes who knew how to obey, who would quickly and efficiently follow orders, were the only ones who lasted. West Point made sure of that. If you question your superiors in a battle situation it can mean not only endangering your life but also placing the whole unit in danger. Do you understand me?"

"I think so," I replied.

"Your boys need to know that you are in charge. You are their commanding officer. It is your job to lead them well and theirs to follow, so that one day they can lead their own troops."

His advice echoes in my ears to this day. With fresh resolve, I turned back to my rambunctious boys, determined to lead well and teach them how to follow. During this training phase, we are giving them the tools they will need to live well and lead others, tools that are increasingly absent in so many young people today.

✟ What Does This Look Like?

It Starts with Parents

Obedience starts with parents. Lovingly and consistently leading our children and teaching them to respectfully obey paves the way for them to have healthy relationships with other realms of authority. We raise kids who will make better employees or bosses, better citizens, better spouses, and better parents when it comes time to raise their own children.

How do we do this? Here are a few places to start:

- ✦ **Make your expectations clear and realistic.** Be specific and have your young pages explain back your instructions so you know they understand.
- ✦ **Remember that training is a process.** Our young charges will not get it the first time. We need to be patient and consistent. Parenthood involves a lot of training—over and over and over again. What you did today, you will need patience to gently train them on *again* tomorrow. But our children's lives are worth this grand investment of time and effort.
- ✦ **Do not expect what you are not willing to inspect.**

Knowing that training takes time, do not tell your child to do something unless you are willing to inspect and make sure it is done. Otherwise they learn that you don't mean what you say.

When we do these things, we begin to create an atmosphere that establishes a *habit* of obedience that leads to a habit of personal discipline that will serve our children well for their whole lives.

Respect for Teachers

Most of us can point to an influential teacher who had a profound effect on our life. Usually it is a teacher who pushed you, would not give up on you, and helped you persevere until you grasped what you were supposed to learn.

Kids who do not learn how to respond appropriately to authority have the distinct disadvantage of missing out on these opportunities. Many a teacher, even those viewed as strict or grouchy, are won over by the respect and willingness of a student to learn.

It used to be that if little Johnny got in trouble at school, the teacher would call the parents. They would work together to establish boundaries and consequences for breeching them. In our current culture this communal act of raising competent, responsible kids is fast disappearing. Parents frequently become defensive, take their child's side, and in the process, undermine their children's ability to mature into responsible adulthood. We have the opportunity to partner with the other adults in our kid's lives and amplify our impact.

Respect for Elders

Wisdom comes with experience and age. That is why cultures all over the world respect and honor those who are older. When we teach our kids to respect their elders, it opens up a world of opportunities for them to glean important life lessons. Teaching our kids to address adults with respect, to listen, and extend courtesy helps our children develop empathy and a respect for the values of life experience. When we can combine the energy of youthful zeal with the wisdom that comes with age, amazing things can happen.

Respect for the Office

Politics have become increasingly volatile in recent years. But we have an opportunity to diffuse tensions and restore a bit of civility. We give our children a great gift when we teach them to respect the office, even—and especially—when we do not agree with the politics.

As a girl, I was invited to apply for a children's committee that would meet with the president of the United States. It was an honor to be invited to apply. Where would I stay? How long would I be there? Would the whole family go back east or would it just be my mom and me? The excitement was palpable. Never once was this president disparaged or was this opportunity belittled. I knew full well that my parents did not agree with many of his political views and decisions. But there was an unwavering respect for the office.

In the days of knights, loyalty was sworn to God and king. Here in the United States, this has morphed into loyalty to God and country. Imagine the impact we can have on our kids if we clearly focus on discussing and debating political views instead of resorting to character assassination.

You and I have a potent opportunity to invest in the future of our country by involving our children in the political process, talking about *why* we hold to some views and not others and communicating respect for governmental offices. That is what my parents accomplished. There were no diatribes, but there was calm, rational debate. And when it came down to it, an invitation to meet the president, no matter his party affiliation, was a high honor.

Learning to obey those in authority over you means respecting the office. A civilized culture survives when there is respect and order. Our republic works because we elect our leaders, and then once elections are over, we work together to see what can be accomplished.

✠ How and When to Say No

Although learning to respect authority is a vital skill our children need to learn, it is also important for them to know when and how to say no to people in perceived or actual authority.

We want to raise children who are independent thinkers instead of mindless followers. They ought to show respect for adults they encounter, but they do not agree with everything an adult says, and they do not necessarily do everything that an adult asks them to do.

How do we teach our kids to disagree appropriately with an authority figure? This training starts at home once a foundation of obedience is in place. As our kids get older it is important that we teach our children when and how to disagree appropriately.

There have been times when my sons have respectfully asked questions about decisions I have made. Sometimes after consideration, I have reevaluated and changed my mind. Here are a few points to remember when teaching your kids what to do when they disagree with a parent or other authority figure:

- ✦ **Teach your young squires that asking questions is more effective than outright disagreeing with someone.** Ask clarifying questions, such as, "Do you mean _____?" "Can you explain why we need to do _____?" "I don't understand why you are asking me to do _____? Wouldn't _____ be a better option?"
- ✦ **Communicate that respect is key.** How your children ask questions is important. Help them learn how to ask questions calmly and respectfully. In our home, whining gets my children nowhere.

- ✦ **Create boundaries.** If your boys start to question everything, it's an indication you need to circle back to respecting and obeying authority again.
- ✦ **Discuss the timing for asking questions.** Teach your children to try to be discreet and ask questions privately. If absolutely necessary have your child say, "I will obey, but could we talk about this later?"

In addition, although we encourage respectful behavior to all and obedience to proper authority, we also train our knights-to-be when and how *not* to obey. There may be times and places when our kids must stand up to an adult and simply, but respectfully, say no.

Carefully define some of the following situations with your children:

You do not go into other people's homes unless your parent has granted permission.

Never go anywhere with another adult without Mom or Dad's explicit, recent permission.

No one (adult or child) should ever have a need to look at or touch your private parts, except for a doctor on rare occasions or a parent if you still need help in the bathroom.

You should never have to do something wrong, such as lie, cheat, or steal, because an adult asks. If you are pressed to do this, go find Mom, Dad, or another trusted adult.

✦ Trust in the Process

This is your castle and your job is to prepare your young charges to someday rule their own realms of influence and authority. They may not understand why, they may not always agree with your decisions, and sometimes you will make mistakes, but your kids need to know that you are there for them. Your job is to prepare them, and theirs is to learn all they can along the way.

It takes time and practice to form any habit. Just as a knight is not born overnight, learning anything—including obedience—takes time. This is about progress, not perfection.

Obedience is essential. When there is a foundation of love and respect in the home, your children can learn to respect others and recognize appropriate authorities in their lives. You must set clear expectations and follow through. As your boys master this habit, they become teachable and ready to undertake the training necessary to become modern-day knights.

✦ Throwing Down the Gauntlet

It is time to throw down the gauntlet and challenge your young charges to grow strong habits of obedience and loyalty. Let's inspire them with the knowledge that we are here to train them to one day rule their own realms, and let's honor the areas in which they are already growing.

✦ **Talk about the idea of realms and domains.** Do your boys understand your role in the home realm to provide, protect, and prepare? Do they understand their own role? Can they identify other realms and the purpose of authority in those realms (workplace, military, government, school, church)?

✦ **Look for examples of obedience and loyalty in daily life.** Examples can also be found in the books you read about knights and the movies you watch. What are the marks of loyalty? When should a knight obey and when should he not?

✦ **Discuss how to show honor and respect in the home.**

- Differentiate between "would you" and "please do." Not everything should be a command. Differentiate between rules that must be obeyed and rules that include flexibility.

- We do not throw food. Make your bed daily. Do not run in the street. (These rules must be obeyed.)

- Get dressed every day. Comb your hair before leaving the house. Read for an hour each afternoon. (These rules offer room for individual style and taste.)

- Teach your boys to respond, "Yes, Mom." Remind them that pages and squires were to learn all they could and obey quickly, completely, without whining or complaining. Reward your kids with verbal affirmation when you notice them starting to do this unprompted.

- Train your young pages to demonstrate they heard the request. "Yes, Mom, I'll obey." "Yes, Dad, I'll do that right away." "Yes, Dad, would it be OK if I swept the floors after I finish this page of homework?"
- Discuss when and how your boys can respectfully disagree.

✦ **Review common courtesies.** Encourage your children to say please, thank you, yes ma'am, and no sir.

✦ **Learn to use honorifics when addressing adults.** Knights of old showed respect for those in authority by using titles of honor, such as King Alfred and Lady Elizabeth. In today's world, that means addressing adults by their appropriate titles, such as Dr. Smith, Pastor Tom, and Miss Jennifer, depending on your community and the individual. Additional honorifics you might want to explain to your boys could include Officer, Judge, General/Colonel/Lieutenant, and the differences between Mrs., Ms., and Miss.

- Role-play meeting some important people. How would they greet the president? You'd look him straight in the eye, give a firm handshake, and say, "Hello, Mr. President."

✦ **Have your boys complete a quest challenge.** Let your kids dress up, if they prefer, and turn obedience practice into a game. Send your young pages and squires on practice quests. You can make this completely silly and fun or weave in some clean-up chores into the process. "Here is your quest, young squire: Find me a red bandana, fight the dragon (stuffed animal), and rescue the princess from that tall tower (the doll up in a tree)." "Transport the enemy soldiers (laundry pile) to the dungeon (washing machine)." Boys always love a challenge. Time them and encourage them to march across the room and pick up everything on the floor. The idea is to keep your voice light and the atmosphere fun and test their ability to follow multiple directions, as Lancelot does in the book *Young Lancelot*.

✦ **Play the whisper game.** This game teaches our children to listen to our voice without our having to raise it. Gather your kids and explain that you are going to call out their names—maybe in a whisper, maybe in a normal voice. The challenge, when called, is to come running, put a hand on your arm, and say, "Yes, Mom." Sometimes call your boy for a purpose and other times just to give him a hug and tell him why you love him so much. This keeps the game element in play while helping him form the habit of coming when you call.

✦ **Play king (queen) says.** Playing the classic Simon Says children's game provides a fun way to practice listening and following directions. To play, someone starts out being the king or queen and gives a command. If he prefaces his command with the words *king says*, the other children must comply (for example, "King says, put your finger on your nose." or "Queen says, jump up and down five times."). If the current king doesn't start by saying the words *king says*, then the other children should not obey. Any child who fails to act when appropriately commanded or acts when he shouldn't have is out of the game. The last child remaining gets to be the next king or queen.

✦ **Assign chores.** Make sure your kids are contributing to the castle upkeep by doing chores. Instruct them to do this cheerfully and *do not pay them*! Expecting them to help around the house should be a part of living there. It builds responsibility and selflessness instead of an entitlement mentality by which they expect us either to do everything for them or to pay them every time they lift their delicate pinkie finger. The goal is to raise tough, resourceful, and responsible boys. See the appendix for ideas of age appropriate chores.

✝ CHAPTER 8

The Code: Stand against Injustice

✝ **_Stand against Injustice and Evil_**

A knight of valor fights against injustice and evil, no matter the personal cost. He recognizes that evil triumphs when good men do nothing and is willing to take that stand to defend and protect those around him.

WAR WHOOPS LET LOOSE from my three boys when I threw out that we would be focusing on the third aspect of the Code of Chivalry: standing against injustice and evil. They tumbled all over each other as they barreled down the stairs jabbering about swords, costumes, and waging imaginary battles.

A knight's chief role is that of protector and defender. Representing the king and his people, he stands ever ready to home in on threats and determine the best ways to defeat them. This vigilant defender of the people lives a life rich with purpose, rife with danger, and replete with unique problems to solve.

If your boys are anything like mine, they will need no help wanting to emulate the physical aspect of the code. They are drawn to these knights of old for precisely this role they play in society. The key for us is to encourage our boys to identify evil in the modern era and be the knights that are so desperately needed in this twenty-first-century world.

There have always been many passionate warriors fighting battles. But not all fight for justice, and not all who honor justice and abhor evil have the courage to do anything about it. What makes a man a hero? What sets him apart from a mere brawler?

A hero embodies the following characteristics:

Moral foundation. Justice is not merely determined by who is in power. A hero is able to identify justice and injustice when he sees it because he has a strong moral foundation that supersedes time and geography.

Strength of character. Doing the right thing becomes a habit, so when it counts most, a boy possesses the inner strength to *do* the right thing.

Strength of mind. Battles are not fought exclusively with physical strength. A hero uses his mind first to develop a strategy of pursuing nonviolent solutions before resorting to force.

Strength of body. A hero develops physical strength and hones skills that enable him to protect and take a stand.

✛ How to Raise Justice-Minded Kids Who Grow Up to Make a Difference

Give Them a Strong Moral Foundation

To fight injustice, boys need to recognize the difference between good and evil. This process starts with giving them a strong foundation in what is good.

Bankers are taught to recognize forgeries not by scanning all of the different kinds of fraudulent money out there but rather by becoming intimately acquainted with the look and feel of real money. Likewise, when we have intimate knowledge and experience with what is good and true and right, we can identify the counterfeit.

Talking to our kids about being fair and truthful, modeling it in our own homes, and pointing out when we see it elsewhere gives our children the grounding to recognize evil automatically. When they learn to value human life and worth, they fight to protect it. When our children are grounded in what is good and true, we can then talk about how to address everything that is wrong. We can model, by our words and actions, how to respond to the injustices we face. This prepares them for their own inevitable en-counters.

For example, every child has an innate sense of what is fair and what is not when it comes to themselves. They are quick to point out when their piece of cake is smaller than their brothers'. But they have not truly internalized justice until we challenge them to divide something fairly them-selves and make sure that each boy gets his due. We talk about how to treat other children justly. We do not hit oth-ers or speak unkindly. We do not belittle or badger. We re-mind them of the words of Daniel Webster who said, "Justice is the ligament which holds civilized beings and civilized nations together."[1]

Stoke the Fire to Fight the Bad Guys

Boys want to be the hero. They want to thwart evil and save the day. Parents stoke the fires of standing against injustice by embracing their son's desire to fight the bad guys. We cultivate this inherent desire when we steep them in the narratives of our historical heroes and of ordinary people who did extraordinary things when faced with the injus-tices of their time. It is in these stories that our boys con-nect with their own potential role in fighting the tyranny they will someday face.

Not only do we read about the time of knights but we fill their minds with the fiery words of Patrick Henry who

---

1. Daniel Webster, speech given at the funeral of Supreme Court Justice Joseph Story, 1845.

stirred people to independence when he said, "Is life so dear or peace so sweet, as to be purchased at the price of chains and slavery? Forbid it, Almighty God! I know not what course others may take; but as for me, give me liberty, or give me death!" We let them stand in awe at the way Thomas Paine influenced patriots everywhere through the profound words penned in his pamphlet *Common Sense* or admire the leadership of George Washington and other military leaders. They learn about Davy Crockett, who lived by the maxim Be Always Sure You Are Right—Then Go Ahead, which led him to confront injustices all throughout his adventurous life, whether it was confronting President Jackson about unjust legislation or his final stand fighting for Texan independence at the Alamo. We teach our sons about Frederick Douglass and Martin Luther King Jr., powerful orators who engaged in the battle to persuasively change hearts and minds about racial injustice. Our boys need to hear these words from King: "The ultimate tragedy is not the oppression and cruelty by the bad people but the silence over that by the good people."

Reading produces empathy. It helps our children imagine themselves in a variety of situations, with all of the thoughts and other emotions that go along with them. It allows them to sense the injustice of a situation that is safely distant from their own struggles. Reading about heroes inspires and empowers them to tackle the problems of their day, knowing they too can be overcome.

We point out everyday heroes we read about in our news feeds, demonstrating that such individuals are needed just as much today as they were in history. Our children can be inspired reading about boys like the members of the fifth-grade football team at a Boston elementary school. Danny Keefe, a friendly six-year-old, loved to wear suits and a fedora to school each day. He also struggled with some speech delays, which drew teasing from fellow classmates. When Tommy Coony heard about the bullying, he told his teammates and they decided to rally around Danny, who often hung out with them, taking on the role of "water coach" for the team. They declared November 20, 2013, Danny Appreciation Day and rallied a total of forty boys to show up to school that day dressed in Danny's dapper fashion.

As our kids get older, we draw their attention to news stories in which people put their very lives on the line to protect others such as when Chris Mintz of Roseburg, Oregon, helped get students at Umpqua Community College to safety before confronting a shooter and surviving, despite being shot seven times.

Boys are built for action. Just as a page would stage battles with his wooden sword, our young charges begin the task of fighting injustice through play, inspired by the heroes they want to emulate. This is not just enjoyable playtime but a powerful exercise that shapes the core of who they will become. After we read about the start of the Revolutionary War, my boys staged regular battles in the backyard, and I would hear each of them, including the three-year-old, shouting out the memorable words of Captain John Parker, "Don't fire unless fired upon, but if they mean to have a war, let it begin here."

Temper Risk Taking with Perspective, but Do Not Tame It

*The young do not know enough to be prudent, and
therefore they attempt the impossible—and achieve it,
generation after generation.*   —*Pearl S. Buck*

Boys love to do crazy stuff; they are risk takers! Many boys come alive at the thought of danger. When my boys were younger, my father would call them with a whisper and a glint in his eye. He would hand them flashlights so they could go hunting for poisonous toads before I could launch into an explanation of neurotoxins. They would come back with chests sticking out and inform me that they "eat danger for breakfast." It was some kind of male ritual and a mantra I still hear them repeat to one another when someone starts to back away from an adventure.

Recently on a hike, I turned around to see my boys staring wide-eyed at a coiled-up copperhead right next to the path. They knew it was a venomous snake right away because of the triangular head shape. One son grabbed a stick, asking if he could poke at it. After I gave him a decisive no, there was an interesting discussion of strike distance (ten to twenty inches) and safety protocol around venomous snakes—important topics when you have three danger-loving boys.

It is our job to temper this youthful characteristic with perspective, but never to tame it. The young have enthusiasm and passion, but perspective comes with age and experience. Tempered with a little bit of wisdom and common sense, taking risks is incredibly beneficial and necessary in a person's life. Boys do not acquire common sense without *some* parental advice.

However, we do not want to squash risk taking. In an age where every little danger is amplified through social media, it can be easy to want to circle the wagons and just keep our children safe. We have visited parks where it is illegal to climb the trees and have experienced other adults giving us dirty looks for allowing the two-year-old to traverse the slide by himself. But could this obsession with reducing risk actually be harming our kids?

According to Dr. Michael Ungar, "Overprotective parenting appears to have become the rule, rather than the exception in today's world and is symptomatic of a new normal, which is causing real harm to children's psychosocial development." He explains that when children are not given the opportunity to take risks in their lives or experience real responsibilities one of two things can happen. Children can develop severe anxiety and long-lasting overdependence on parents and/or they can become rebellious as they try to prove that they can face risks they were never prepared to handle in the first place.[2] Our sons need the chance to test their wings, and we need to give them the freedom to fail earlier rather than later.

As a mother of boys, one of my goals in parenting is to

2. Michael Ungar, "The Perils of Overprotective Parenting," *Psychotherapy Networker* (September–October 2014). Available at psychotherapynetworker.org/magazine/article/80/bubble-wrapping-our-children.

raise them to be calculated risk takers—*balancing initiative with wisdom*. That means we step in and intervene at times, especially if the consequences could be life threatening. Other times we stand back and let them try, even if it means they will fail or get physically hurt on a small scale.

Teach Them the Power of One

One barrier to standing against injustice is paralysis in the face of evil. Known as the bystander effect, this psychosociological phenomenon makes people less inclined to help when others are present because they assume someone else will intervene, their actions cannot make a difference, or the risk of action is too great to their own safety.

The antidote to this phenomenon is telling your boys that they have a responsibility to act, no matter what.

As Edmund Burke said, "The only thing necessary for the triumph of evil is for good men to do nothing." My husband and I tell our boys, in no uncertain terms, that we expect them to stand for justice, even if they stand alone. And that is, after all, the trick to overcoming the bystander effect—realizing that it exists and making a conscious decision to compensate for it.

I also tell them a tale of two trains that played out only a month apart.

Kevin Sutherland, a recent college graduate, was murdered while riding the Washington, D.C., Metro on July 4, 2015. The *Washington Post* reported that "passengers trapped in the moving train huddled at both ends of the car and watched in horror" as the attack took place, doing nothing to stop it.[3] What started out as a robbery attempt quickly escalated when Jasper Spires started kicking and stabbing Sutherland some thirty or forty times before exiting the subway train at the next stop. Why did no one intervene when a combined effort by just a few of the passengers could have saved Sunderland's life? One man shared his reflections on why he did not step in to stop the attack, saying, "What I don't wish is that I had somehow tried to attack the assailant. I am a little bit larger than he was, but I would not have won. It's scary, because if we had been sitting closer and had seen the attack start I probably would have tried to help, and would have been stabbed."

Why did people not step in to help?

✦ Fear: What if I get hurt?
✦ Helplessness: I do not know what to do.
✦ Confusion: Because no one else is doing anything, maybe everything is OK.
✦ Hope: I'm sure someone official will take care of it.

Another experience on a train outside of Paris just a month later had a far different outcome.

A Frenchman made his way to the restroom when he came face to face with a bare-chested man brandishing

3. Peter Hermann, Michael Smith, and Keith L. Alexander, "Horrified Passengers Witnessed Brutal July 4 Slaying aboard Metro Car," *Washington Post*, July 7, 2015. Available at washingtonpost.com/local/crime/victim-in-metro-slaying-stabbed -repeatedly-during-robbery-on-train/2015/07/07/8dd09132-249b-11e5-b72c -2b7d516e1e0e_story.html?tid=a_inl.

weapons. Instead of running for cover, he attempted to disarm the assailant. His attempt failed, but it inspired a fifty-one-year-old English professor to wrestle an AK-47 away from the attacker before he was shot in the scuffle. Those shots woke up three young American men who quickly assessed the situation and together took on the attacker and disarmed him, ultimately saving many lives.

Each of these men were heroes. They stepped up and did something when evil reared its ugly head. But it started with one person, which led to another and then finally to three more, who were able to successfully take down the terrorist due to their quick thinking and willingness to help.

Opportunities to overcome the bystander effect and stand against injustice are everywhere. Helping our kids connect these stories to scenarios they might face is essential. When we first started knight training my three boys were three, four, and six. I overheard one of my sons intervening when the other was picking on the three-year-old saying, "Stop. That is not fair. Be the good guy instead."

✠ Throwing Down the Gauntlet

No matter how old our boys are, we can cast a vision, throwing down the gauntlet and challenging our boys to embody this quintessential aspect of knighthood. Opportunities abound to help prepare them to effectively and subconsciously step in when the need arises.

♦ **Foundations.** What is justice? Injustice? What do we base our standards of right and wrong on? See if your children can explain that to you. Make a habit of having ongoing conversations about how to discern right from wrong and what should guide them in making these determinations.

♦ **Read.** Make a list of narrative books with heroic role models and have your kids pick a few to read in the next couple of weeks. Talk about what the heroes in the books did and how they were brave. For your older boys, make another list of books that teach about justice. After reading them, discuss. Examples are religious texts such as the Bible (Proverbs or Romans), the "Letter from Birmingham Jail" or other writings from Martin Luther King Jr., William Bennett's *Book of Virtue*, and Thomas Paine's *Common Sense*.

♦ **Pretend.** If your child needs some inspiration and prompting for imaginative play, come up with some medieval scenarios in which one would fight injustice. Demonstrate what a strong and valiant knight would do. He might rescue someone from a dragon or defeat a group of rascally robbers on a forest path or engage in a battle to defend his castle. Encourage and make time for spontaneous, child-directed play so your kids can work out for themselves what it means to be the hero.

♦ **Role-play.** Ask your child what kind of situations one might encounter in today's world in which he could take a stand against injustice. Talk about how one might handle them and role-play (for example, sibling arguments, picking on someone at home, school, or play, catching a friend stealing something).

✦ **Wielding words.** Help your sons see that many times fighting against injustice happens without the use of traditional weapons. They need to know that the pen is mightier than the sword, that persuasive speech can be even more powerful because it can turn even enemies into allies. The need for these justice warriors is always with us, and the possibilities for conquering evil and injustice are endless. Ask your older kids to write a persuasive letter to the editor or your local newspaper.

✦ **Talk.** Explain the bystander effect and regularly review the importance of resisting it. Telling your young pages about the two trains that I mentioned in this chapter can be an excellent starting point. As you engage in discussion, be mindful of your boys' ages and personality when deciding how much to tell them. The purpose is to inspire them, not to fill them with fear. My boys were eight, ten, and twelve at the time. I would have simply waited or relayed a much abbreviated version had they been younger.

✦ **Situational awareness.** Developing situational awareness is vital for any knight who wants to be ready to step in and save the day. This enables him to remain calm and confident in stressful situations in which he might be called on to help. We need to challenge our young pages and squires to become aware of their surroundings.

- Beginner situational awareness: An excellent place to start building situational awareness skills is street and parking lot safety. Ask your kids what they should look and listen for when crossing the street (cars, bicycles, the sound of car engines, etc.). What should they watch for in a parking lot (taillights, people getting into cars, etc.)? Although these examples are safety focused, they will help your boys develop the observation skills needed to recognize situations in which they will be called on to help.
- Situational awareness challenge. When you are out and about, periodically stop for a situational awareness challenge. Have your boys close their eyes and see if they can tell you *who, what, when, where,* or *how* of their current environment. Where are they? Can they name the restaurant, describe the location? How did they get there? How could they get home, to their car, out of the building? Where are the exits? Who is around them, how many are there, and can they describe any of them? The key is to make it a fun challenge. When you are just starting out, focus on building one aspect of awareness at a time.
- Play guess who? Learn how to describe people by homing in on hair color, eye color, height, and so on.
- Play memory or concentration and hone observation and memory skills by finding matches.
- Read the I Spy! books.

CHAPTER 9

The Code: Protect the Weak

> ✝ *Defend and Protect the Weak*
>
> A noble knight is always on the lookout for someone who needs help. When he sees someone in need, he steps in and does whatever is necessary to help in the situation.

"IS IT TRUE that I can really have two hearts, Mommy?" my youngest son asked. We were settling in for some special time together and his book of choice yet again was *Young Lancelot.* We have read this book more times than I can count. It tells the story of Lancelot's childhood and how he came to be one of the greatest knights of the Round Table.

I do not mind reading him this story for the bazillionth time because each and every time, I see him processing it again, internalizing the valuable lessons so beautifully communicated in this book. He learns that the strength of a man is not merely physical. This is the story of how a young, unbelievably talented knight in training learns to trade in pride and arrogance for humility and goodness.

> *"A knight needs two hearts," the lady of the lake told him. "One should be hard as a diamond when battling cruelty and injustice. The other should be soft as warm wax to respond to goodness and gentleness."*
>
> *Lancelot scoffed at the idea of a knight moved by tenderness. "A warrior must be strong inside and out," he insisted. "I want only a heart that is diamond-hard."*

With luscious illustrations and beautiful text, we encounter the journey of discovery that makes a man a true knight. Lancelot sets off on many adventures and performs heroic deeds in fighting against injustice and evil, but it is not until he learns empathy, until he discovers compassion that he truly comes into his own. This little boy of mine is listening with rapt attention as Lancelot discovers that he must "become a knight who is both brave and generous, who will serve the mightiest king or the weakest of the weak."

We close the book, and my son is off, grabbing his sword, snagging a playsilk cape, and trotting outdoors. He is Lancelot—taking on giants, fighting back foes, and developing both hearts as he tenderly reaches down to grab a teddy bear and bring it to safety.

Young Lancelot beautifully illustrates a key difference between a chivalrous knight and any other kind of warrior. For a truly great knight, compassion and courage go hand in hand. He is not arrogant and violent but rather uses his strength for the greater good.

This required no didactic lessons from me. In fact, I wonder if this would have lost its impact had I tried to implement a clear lesson. My youngest boy simply marinated in the message of the narrative by reading it over and over again, allowing it to fill his imagination and shape his moral character. As situations arose, I gently pointed out the opportunities he had to follow in Lancelot's footsteps, to extend compassion and help to someone in need—whether it was a sibling with an owie needing a bandage or a lonely child at our weekly park outing who needed a friend.

The concept of compassion and empathy wove its way through the entirety of chivalrous thought. Geoffroi de Charny wrote about this in his twelfth-century book on chivalry, "They should be humble among their friends, proud and bold against their foes, tender and merciful toward those who need assistance, pleasant and amiable with all others."[1]

From the *Song of Roland*, we are inspired to protect the weak and defenseless and to give succor to widows and orphans. Charlemagne lays this out even more clearly in the exhortation he gave in A.D. 800 when he was crowned emperor of the Holy Roman Empire. His words were aimed to

---

1. Geoffroi de Charny, *A Knight's Own Book of Chivalry* (Philadelphia: University of Pennsylvania Press, 2005), p. 70.

his sons and his top knights—those in leadership. He charged them to do ill to no man, to help the oppressed, and to defend the cause of the widow and orphan.

Léon Gautier, the renowned nineteenth-century French historian, summed up this chivalric ideal thus: "Thou shalt respect all weaknesses and shalt constitute thyself the defender of them."[2]

It was this ethos that truly set a valiant knight apart from just an ordinary soldier. Knights were to be warriors, yes, but never because they preyed on the weak. There was no honor in victory that came at the expense of taking advantage of others. A true knight was a protector of the people.

✝ Cultivating the Seeds of Compassion

Little boys, our knights in training, are oftentimes rough and tumble one moment and then tender and sweet the next. Boys roar, embody wild, and awe us with their imaginative spirit. But they can be surprisingly intuitive sometimes, giving you that comforting hug just when you need it, caring for a younger child, or rescuing that injured bird they discovered.

What could happen if we choose to celebrate everything that makes them uniquely boy? If we delighted in their rough-and-tumble play, setting boundaries for their loud and boundless energy without squashing it, and cultivating

2. Léon Gautier, *Chivalry* (London: George Rutledge and Sons, 1891), translated by Henry Frith, p. 26.

their sweet hearts that want to protect others? By turning their hearts and minds toward the ideals of chivalry, we are able to celebrate our boys and cultivate the very best in them in a way that prepares them to make an impact within their families and the community.

Our culture simply wants them to sit still, to be calmer, to be tame. Boys are diagnosed as defective when they do not act more like little girls and, sadly, sometimes drugged to bring them to this calm, subdued state of being. This might make life easier for parents and teachers, but we do so at the expense of taking that light out of our sons' eyes and the fire out of their spirits. We deaden the drive to live a life of meaning and impact.

Our boys are just as capable of compassion and tenderness, but it will look different from the way it does for our girls. For starters, it will be a whole lot more active. We want to inspire them to use their exuberant energy and boundless enthusiasm to pursue these chivalric ideals, to rescue and help everyone they encounter.

✠ How Do We Cultivate Compassion?

Provide Stability

Although the seeds of empathy are in each of our children, careful cultivation is needed. We do this by providing children with a stable, nurturing home and relationships. When their needs are met, they are more likely to rise to meet the needs of others because it has been modeled to them. We help them develop compassion by reading to them. We see that the number of stories preschoolers hear predict their ability to understand the emotions of others and that adults who read less fiction also appear to be less empathetic as well.[3] Talking to our kids in the everyday moments of life allows us to build an awareness for the needs of others. Giving our children time to play so they can practice this kind of rescuing, protecting, and defending in a safe, relaxed atmosphere helps them internalize these values.

Inspire Them with a Sense of Purpose

We cultivate compassion by casting vision and filling their minds with a sense of purpose. Being brave, being strong does not just happen when they "fight the bad guys." It happens when they spot any kind of need and step in to help. Our boys have the opportunity each and every day to be a hero to someone. What is a hero? It is simply an average person doing the extraordinary thing of putting the needs of others before his own safety or comfort. It entails taking risks in his effort to problem solve. In other words, this involves doing what our boys are wired to do so well! As they become aware of their surroundings and the needs of others, they have opportunities to take action.

---

3. R. Mar, J. Tackett, and C. Moore, "Exposure to Media and Theory-of-Mind Development in Preschoolers," *Cognitive Development* 25 (2010): 69–78.

Inspire Them to Lead the Way

Taking up the mantle of knighthood means being a leader. A knight does not wait for others to take action, he inspires others to follow him as he steps in and leads the way toward helping those around him. Our knights in training need to be reminded of the power of the bystander effect. Human nature stands by, watching and waiting for direction. This diffusion of responsibility can have serious effects when individuals are not motivated to take action. But our boys are not average people. They are defenders and protectors of humanity. They are never passive watchers but rather are men of action who quickly take stock of the situation and step in to help.

Inspire Them by Recognizing and Valuing Their Strength

Boys beam when we recognize and appreciate their strength. When we acknowledge their physical contributions to helping others, we are solidifying the fact that their strength is valued and needed. "Wow! Check out those muscles! I'm so glad you are so strong and helping me to pull all of these weeds." "You are so strong. Thank you for helping Grandma move that chair to the other side of the room."

But strength does not just reside only in our muscles. A true knight is strong in body, spirit, and heart. He has the physical strength to get things done, the spirit and drive to take the risks needed to step into these spaces to help, and the heart that feels empathy for those that need it. As parents, we can help our boys home in on their secret strength—compassion. For Lancelot, this was his "second heart," the heart that could imagine what it would be like to walk in someone else's shoes, the heart that does not want others to suffer if it is in his power to do something to alleviate it, the heart that is so moved that it will do whatever it takes to help. Compassion is empathy in action.

Studies reveal that having this kind of empathy is key to overcoming the bystander effect that so easily cripples us into inaction. When our kids can put themselves in another person's shoes, they are more likely to take action to alleviate the problem.[4]

Just as we are unpacking the vital importance of empathy in fueling compassionate action, recent studies also reveal that this kind of empathy is declining among young people, with a dramatic drop in the last ten years.[5] To make matters worse, the simultaneous growth in students' self-reported narcissism has reached new heights, according to research by Jean M. Twenge, a psychologist at San Diego State University.[6] Selfishness paralyzes people from pursuing any action that is not a direct benefit to oneself. A narcissist will still occasionally dabble in altruism, as Lancelot initially did

4. Nicola Abbot and Lindsey Cameron, "What Makes a Young Assertive Bystander? The Effect of Intergroup Contact, Empathy, Cultural Openness, and In-Group Bias on Assertive Bystander Intervention Intentions," *Journal of Social Issues* 70 (2014): 167–82.

5. Jamil Zaki, "What, Me Care? Young Are Less Empathetic," *Scientific American*, January 1, 2011. Available at scientificamerican.com/article/what-me-care.

6. J. M. Twenge and W. K. Campbell, *The Narcissism Epidemic: Living in the Age of Entitlement* (New York: Atria Books, 2010).

in the book *Young Lancelot*, but they do it for their own glory, not out of any true concern for others. We do not need kids who help for the sake of a self-congratulating selfie, but rather kids who step in to save the day because it is the right thing to do, even if no one else seems to notice.

We want our boys to know that the strength of a man is found in protecting the weak. We need to raise a generation of men who will continue to protect the vulnerable and step in to save the day. It is a role that our boys are perfectly suited to take up, no matter their age. This kind of strength is developed through repetition so that it becomes his default mode. And when this strength is fully formed, it is contagious, inspiring others to follow suit.

✣ Pave the Way by Setting the Example

It was a hot, dusty day one Arizona spring when I piled into my friend Anna's station wagon with her family, excited to head out for a fun day and probably even more excited about sitting in the backward-facing third row where we would spend the trip trying to get people in cars behind us to either honk or wave. But our backseat shenanigans came to an abrupt stop when her dad pulled over. "Just a quick stop, kids," Mr. Heller called out. I groaned inside, looking around to see how my friend and her brothers were taking the news of the stop. They were all craning their necks and looking to see what their dad was doing. I followed Anna's example and unbuckled so I could get a peek at what was unfolding. Her dad had walked over and after a brief conversation with a woman stranded by the side of the road, he proceeded to change her flat tire. This was before the age of cell phones, and there were no people nearby. This woman was truly stranded out in the Arizona heat until this knight in shining armor showed up. He had not even thought twice about stopping to help. For all of my initial disappointment about being late, I have no recollection of where we were actually going that day. I remember it being hot, but really have no memory of feeling discomfort sitting in the warm car. What I do remember is that Mr. Heller stopped, even though it was not convenient.

Like the knights of old, pulling over to help was not a conscious decision, but a result of who my friend's father had become: someone who enthusiastically helps anyone in need. That enthusiasm and ready-for-action attitude was contagious. He raised four boys and a girl who embody that chivalrous spirit with everyone they encounter.

We can talk all we want to our children about what they should do, but are we living it? Our children absorb our behavior, the words we use, and the actions we take. If we want to raise heroic children who put the needs of others before their own and are ready to step in to make a difference, we need to be modeling that ourselves. We need to embrace the beauty and power of living out life side by side with our children and realize that life's greatest lessons are learned from the examples of others.

Our boys catch the vision when we inspire them with stories from the past, with the adventure and purpose that helping others provides, and letting them see this adventure play out in our own lives.

✠ Everyday Knight in Shining Armor

"They're here, they're here!" my boys shrieked. The two bigger boys tore around the corner in a race for the front door, both eager to help. Little Treyton toddled after them aware that something exciting was happening and eager to be a part of the action. My sister had arrived with her two kids. As she wrangled the infant seat out of the car, my two boys arrived and breathlessly asked if they could help carry things in for her. With only a hint of a smile, she thanked them profusely for coming to the rescue and handed them a few bags to carry. My oldest beamed as he strutted in with a diaper bag slung over his shoulder and a bag full of groceries.

They felt strong and needed, knowing that they played an important role in the events unfolding at the moment. And this is the gift we want to give our boys. We want to inspire them to look for ways to help. We want to appreciate and acknowledge when their strength is put to use helping others. Because even young boys want to live a life of purpose. They want to make a difference. They want to be treated as men, worthy of honor and respect.

Cultivating these moments of manhood-in-the-making is magical. Inspiring our boys with purpose and vision that will carry them through as they make a habit of coming to the rescue, of spotting a need, and stepping in to help. We all benefit as they step into this role of knights in shining armor.

Could my sister have handled getting everything in on her own? Definitely. But with a baby and toddler to juggle, she was in a place where help was definitely appreciated.

It is critical that we make helping others a priority in our own lives as well as in the lives of our children. Everyday simple actions become habits that shape the character of who our children will become. As education philosopher Charlotte Mason puts it, "Every day, every hour, the parents are either passively or actively forming those habits in their children upon which, more than upon anything else, future character and conduct depend."

Faithfulness in the everyday moments prepares our boys for those pivotal junctures they might face. While folding laundry one day, my friend Jamie Mehan watched a riveting scene unfold on the TV screen. She paused the action to call her boys into the room. Eleven-year-old Sam ambled in with his younger brothers to watch as a man held out his arms to shield a woman holding a baby. Jamie paused it and turned to her boys, "*That* is what a man does. He protects others. He is placing himself between danger and that woman and her baby." She hit play again and the boys discovered that he was face to face with a tiger. Softly, the man in the movie whispered, "When he lunges for me, run." Wide-eyed the boys took it all in wondering if they could do something similar should the need arise.

Sam did not have long to wait for just such an opportunity. Several families went on a camping trip, and Sam was running around with his friends. What they did not realize was that a six-year-old boy was doing his very best to keep up with the big boys. As this little guy shifted his weight to follow them up an incline near the creek, the ground gave way and he slid down and into the water. The icy water flowed fast and was far too deep for him to stand up. The older boys, hearing the scream and splash, came running to see what happened. With only a moment's pause, Sam jumped in, swimming quickly to where the boy was being swept downstream, struggling to keep his head above water. The boy latched on to him as Sam fought to plant his feet on the one high point in the midst of the swiftly moving creek where he could keep their heads above water. The others went for help. Sam's dad soon arrived and swam out to help get the little boy to safety. As the day unfolded, the men in their group came over to high-five Sam and the mothers plied him with treats. He was a little confused and bashful at all the attention. His mother walked over, cupping his face in her hands told him, "*This* is what it means to be a man. Your quick thinking saved that boy's life." In that split second when a decision needed to be made, he made it. A calm confidence overtook him as he walked tall the rest of the day. When the need arose, he had proved his mettle. He had the makings of a man.

When recognizing the needs of others and valiantly stepping in to help becomes a habit, it becomes enjoyable and effortless. This was the case with my friend's dad. He did not even hesitate to think about whether or not to help.

Helping was his default mode, and each of his children followed in his footsteps. When we challenge our boys to protect the weak, they too step up into these important roles.

Compassion in action is the key that Lancelot needed to learn. He needed to begin to understand that there was purpose outside of merely pursuing glory and honor for self in serving a mighty king. In our picture book reading, Lancelot set out on a final quest initially for glory—to prove he was the greatest knight of all, even though he despised the person he was called on to help. The battle he engaged in was a battle of the heart and mind. He could not overcome it through physical strength alone. It was not until he reached the point of giving up that he finally started to feel empathy and think through what his inaction would mean for his fellow knight who was on death's door or for that man's sister who had tearfully begged Lancelot to take on this last quest to save her brother's life. Lancelot realized he must take action because the lives of others, the feelings of others were at stake. It was only when his motivation shifted from self-glory to helping others that he gained victory. True greatness is found in serving others, in standing up for the weakest of the weak, in recognizing the needs and feelings of others.

We can help our boys realize this true greatness by reading great books to them and giving them time for free play to pretend to be that hero. We need to refrain from always stepping in and directing their play and instead allow them to work out the ideals of service on their own. Finally, we help them grow in empathy and service by talking to them about the situations they encounter and modeling everyday knighthood through our own actions. We solidify these lessons by challenging our boys to pursue ample practice so that this aspect of knighthood becomes not just what they do but who they have become.

✦ Throwing Down the Gauntlet

- **Read, read, read.** In your read-aloud time, point out the characters who help others and talk about how people feel when they are in situations in which they need help. Connect your kids with the feelings people feel after they are helped or after they help others. (This works for movies too.)
- **Provide time for pretend play.** Provide time in your child's schedule for play, especially after you have read stories. If they need a nudge to get started, enter into their pretend play. Encourage them to rescue, protect, and defend.
- **Role-play.** Role-play situations in which your child can help someone else (picking up something that has fallen, opening the door for an elderly or disabled person, carrying bags for someone, rescuing a hurt animal, helping a lonely child at school sitting by themselves).
- **Help your boy become an everyday knight in shining armor.** Make these suggestions:

- Watch over those who are younger than you. Be careful to not be too rough and hurt younger kids when playing around them.
- Play with someone younger. You will make his day!
- Sit with another kid who looks lonely at school, home, or the park.
- Help elderly neighbors or relatives: water their plants, get their mail, take out their trash.
- Return someone's shopping cart for her at the store.
- Offer to carry bags or books for someone.
- Open doors for others, especially those carrying a heavy load or the elderly or disabled.

✦ **Teach basic first-aid.** Teach your kids how to clean and bandage a wound.

✦ **Stress situational awareness.** Just as they used situational awareness to spot danger and take a stand against injustice, our boys can use it to identify when someone needs help. Charge your young squires to be on the lookout for those who need help.

✦ **Practice positive affirmations.** Have your kids repeat this affirmation: "I'm always on the lookout for ways to help." Let your young page know that, even when they don't specifically ask for help, people count on him because he is a knight (in training).

✦ **Volunteer.** Find local opportunities to help those in

need as a family. It could be packaging up shoes to be sent to children who have none, serving food at a homeless shelter, or preparing food packs to go to impoverished areas around the globe.

✦ **Practice reading emotions.** Many boys do not intuitively pick up on this and will need a parent to gently guide them on how to read emotions and react accordingly. Ask questions, such as these: "How do you think he feels right now?" "Why might he feel that way?" You can practice by looking at pictures in magazines, engaging in people watching at a busy shopping area or park, or talking in the midst of interactions our children are having with others. "Why is your sister crying right now? How does this make her feel?" "Could she have reacted angrily because she is really feeling sad? How can you help her?"

✛ CHAPTER 10

The Code: Respect Women

✛ *Respect and Honor Women*

A valiant knight holds women in high regard and seeks to show them honor by treating them as fellow human beings and giving respect by acknowledging their unique strengths.

PERHAPS NOTHING COMMUNICATES CHIVALRY more than the ideas behind how a man treats a woman. The roots for this run deep within history.

The chivalric code called knights to a higher purpose. They viewed themselves as protectors and defenders. The very way they carried themselves and how they treated others immediately set them apart from the average man.

The Kitchen Knight, one of my favorite picture books, tells the story of Gareth of Orkney, nephew to King Arthur. He arrived at Camelot and served in the kitchen for a year before partially revealing himself and setting out with a grand lady, Lady Linette, on a quest to free her sister from the captivity of a rogue knight. This proud woman was mortified that a mere kitchen boy would be assigned to rescue her sister. She treated him with contempt and utter rudeness. Through it all he kept his cool, despite her continued taunts and belittling demands that he flee to save his own life. When he remained respectful yet steadfast, she broke, ashamed of her behavior because she recognized his true greatness. He did not waver or badger her back. He also did not abandon the quest but stuck by his word. In everything he carried himself with inner strength and even showed quiet respect when none was deserved. Lady Linette responded, "What manner of man are you! Never did a woman treat a knight so shamefully as I have you, and you have always answered me courteously. Only a man of noble blood would do so."

This is a common thread seen within medieval literature. A knight (or noble lady) was recognized not by what they wore or who they declared themselves to be but by how they conducted themselves around others. There was a dignity and a respect for themselves as well as for others that set them apart.

As we challenge our boys in their quest to become modern-day knights we want to instill in them the habits of treating others, especially the women in their lives, with love, respect, and courtesy.

There is a popular saying that goes, "Being male is a

matter of birth. Being a man is a matter of age. But being a gentleman is a matter of choice."[1] Our desire is to make this choice of gentlemanly behavior such an ingrained habit that it becomes second nature. Aristotle called this habituating virtue.[2]

Everyone recognizes the problems we have with how men and women relate to one another these days. We have lost that mutual respect. We do not change this unfortunate reality by reacting according to how we are treated, but rather with how we *ought* to treat one another. When my children bicker, I frequently remind them that it takes two to fight and one to start making progress toward peace. Just like our boys have the opportunity to embrace the power of one when standing against injustice or protecting the weak, they can lead the way in creating an atmosphere in which men and women respect one another. They can be the Kitchen Knight.

✝ Of Respect and the Rescue

"Stand back, my lady. I'll battle that (stuffed animal) dragon," my young one bellowed as he looked over his shoulder to make sure I was watching from a safe distance. Boys long for the allure of battles to wage, and fair maidens (or moms) to rescue. The women in his life play a critical role, and he

---

1. Some Internet sources attribute this to Vin Diesel, others say unknown.
2. Aristotle, *Nicomachean Ethics*, Book II (Oxford: Oxford University Press, 2009), p. xx.

will do just about anything for those he loves and he wants you to know it.

John Eldridge says, "deep in his heart, every man longs for a battle to fight, an adventure to live, and a beauty to rescue."[3] This is evident in even our youngest boys. How often do we hear, "Mom, Mom, watch this!" as he heroically grabs a rope and jumps off the swing set? Long before hormones kick in, he wants to impress that woman in his life. And for now that woman is you, Mom.

It does not take long for the protective instinct to kick it up a notch. My oldest son was nine or ten when he overheard his father and me reminiscing about our once-upon-a-time courtship days and how he would always slip behind and around me to take up the position of walking along the street, putting himself between me and traffic. At the time it was simultaneously confusing and yet so attractive to experience that protective move each time we walked together.

Without a word on our next walk, my son slipped around to take up the position next to the street. While my protective mama bear instinct wanted to switch places to shield *him* from harm, I realized that he was processing what it meant to be a man and he knew that protecting me was his top priority.

We challenge our boys to show courtesy toward ladies by opening doors, giving up their seats, and taking up the protective position along the curb not because women are

---

3. John Eldridge, *Wild at Heart: Discovering the Secret of a Man's Soul* (Nashville: Thomas Nelson Publishing, 2001), p. 9.

weak, but rather as an acknowledgment of their inherent worth and dignity.

Just as the ladies of the castle would shape the moral foundation for a young page, mothers today have the opportunity to delight in his boyish antics and desire to impress while helping develop his second heart, which expresses empathy and recognizes the dignity and worth of others. While a boy wants to protect his mama, he usually wants to be like his dad. A father sets the example without even having to utter a word. His actions speak loudly and the boy hears it.

✦ Respect Goes Both Ways

Teaching respect begins by recognizing sameness before differences. Our boys must recognize that the similarities of male and female far outweigh the differences. We are all people. For a medieval knight, this respect was rooted in the idea of the Imago Dei. We need to raise boys who value women as people. Every person is uniquely created and worthy of honor and respect simply because he or she is human. This has nothing to do with others' looks, their behavior, what they might do for you, or how they contribute to society.

This idea is foundational. We cannot cultivate our sons' protective instincts toward the women in their life without instilling the idea that women have intrinsic value.

We eschew the idea that girls (or boys) have cooties; we

discourage play from devolving into boys versus girls. We promote the value of friendships with boys and girls, especially in the first ten years of a child's life. Girls and boys both have fantastic thoughts and ideas. They have unique feelings and interests. We want our boys to recognize the value in having positive friendships with girls.

However, boys and girls are different, especially in how we communicate. Boys will roughhouse, belch, and throw around smack talk. Part of honoring women is showing care and respect. We help our boys realize that women and girls, in general, do not like that kind of relating. Boys bond over smack talk. Girls do not. Boys wrestle each other to the ground as a way of showing affection. Girls do not.

Boys want to be strong. In fact, biology predisposes them to possessing greater strength than a woman. It is a simple matter of testosterone. This greater physicality can be used for good when respect is present or it can be used for horrific evil when it is absent.

Girls and women tend to be more intuitive and empathetic, often assuming men and boys are also highly empathetic. This has caused many a misunderstanding between the sexes throughout history. Although it can be frustrating to curtail our boys' pure physicality and to teach them how to discuss feelings and navigate the more obvious emotional differences between them and girls, giving them the ability to recognize the strengths these skills afford is invaluable.

We have the opportunity to help our young kids establish the knowledge and skills needed to relate to the opposite sex before hormones make it extra challenging. We do this not only by helping our kids understand where they are similar but also by helping them recognize and see the value in their differences as we traverse the ever sticky realm of relationships.

A while back, I was taking a photo of my niece when her brother came bounding in, trying to hijack the picture with goofy faces and bunny ears. A scowl and a "please stop" from my niece fell on deaf ears.

"You are trying to make this a silly picture aren't you? Do you like it when you or your friends look funny in pictures?" I asked.

My nephew nodded eagerly.

I hunched down, speaking in a hushed voice as they both leaned close.

"Well, I'm going to let you in on a secret. Girls typically don't like that. It is practically a universal law. Women do not like having bad pictures of themselves. Isn't that right?" I said, turning to my niece.

Her eyes widened as I nailed her feelings of frustration. This afforded an opportunity to help my young nephew understand a bit of the female psyche. It helped him see why his sister protested and why I asked him to stop. Tiny conversations like this play a role in the daily training of our men-in-the-making because it helps clue them in on how they can show respect for women even though they do not share the same feelings.

✠ Women As People or Women As Objects?

With college rape in the news and domestic violence rates high, there is no greater time than now to teach boys to respect and honor women. We can and we must raise boys who are of a different ilk. They need to understand that it is never OK to degrade the dignity of another human being. We should never be that parent who justifies a son's heinous crimes as merely "twenty minutes of action" because, as Ann Voskamp puts it, "When the prevailing thinking is boys will be boys—girls will be garbage."[4]

One of the most obvious threats to helping our boys grow to honor and respect women is the sex-saturated culture we live in. It fills the media we consume, the billboards we see; it calls out to us from the check-out aisle in the grocery store and is rampant on the Internet.

If we do not address the realities of the culture we live in with our children, the default will be to embrace it as normal. When we focus solely on the body and sexual appetites, we lose sight of the soul.

But how do we fight this? How do we protect the dignity of women who are objectified and reduced to just a body and how do we protect the dignity of a man—of our boys—

---

4. Ann Voskamp, "About those '20 Minutes of Action': 20 Things We'd Better Tell Our Sons Right Now About Being Real Men," *Ann Voskamp*, June 8, 2016. Available at aholyexperience.com/2016/06/about-those-20-minutes-of-action-20-things-wed -better-tell-our-sons-right-now-about-being-real-men.

so that they know that they are more than the sum of their sexual appetites?

It starts early. It starts by modeling what healthy male–female relationships look like. It begins by helping them form healthy friendships with girls. It means having conversations, sometimes awkward ones, with our boys over and over again.

We also need to address the elephant in the room: pornography. We can decry rape culture, but we must realize that this did not materialize out of nowhere. Rape culture exists because of the undercurrent of rampant porn culture.

Dr. Michael Flood, a research professor in Australia reports, "There is consistent evidence that exposure to pornography is related to male sexual aggression against girls and women. . . . In a recent longitudinal study of U.S. youth aged 10 to 15, with three waves of data over three years, individuals who intentionally consumed violent X-rated materials were over *six times* as likely as others to engage in sexually aggressive behavior" (emphasis added).[5]

Thanks to the Internet, pornography is now easier to access than ever. One does not even have to go looking for it. It will find you. Hal and Melanie Young speak to thousands of families each year about raising boys, and the stories they hear from good parents who discover that their

---

5. Michael Flood, "Inquiry into the Harm Being Done to Australian Children through Access to Pornography on the Internet," submission to the Australian Parliament, March 10, 2016. Available at xyonline.net/sites/default/files/Flood,%20Senate%20submission%202016_0.pdf.

sweet boys are ensnared in the tentacles of an online pornography habit are gut wrenching. Increasingly, they hear
from loving, involved parents who have boys as young as
six and seven who are already hooked on pornography.
Their advice: (1) Lay the foundation for virtue and right
thinking early in your child's life. (2) Be on the lookout for
situations in which your children might be exposed to pornography. (3) Equip your children to say no to the allure of
pornography.

Getting an accurate idea of how many young boys are
viewing pornography is challenging. Researchers primarily
must rely on survey studies of college students to ascertain
how early pornography exposure begins. One 2008 study
found that 93 percent of boys and 62 percent of girls were
exposed to online pornography during adolescence and
that boys were more likely to be exposed at an earlier age, to
see far more, and to form a pornography habit.[6] Another
survey revealed that a quarter of all exposure to pornography occurred before puberty.[7] Because these studies were
conducted before the prevalence of smartphones and tablets, researchers and therapists warn that the numbers are
much higher today, which is a hard pill to swallow when we
are looking at our sweet young boys.

Here are a few ways we can empower our kids to *reject*
the pull of pornography:

---

6. C. Sabin, J. Wolak, and D. Finkelhor, "The Nature and Dynamics of Internet
Pornography Exposure for Youth," *Cyberpsychology and Behavior* 11, no. 6 (2008):
691–93.
7. David Kinnaman, "The Porn Phenomenon," Barna, February 5, 2016. Available
at barna.com/the-porn-phenomenon/#.

Define Pornography in Simple Terms

✦ For a young child, talk about modesty and the importance of avoiding looking at pictures of people without their clothes on.

✦ For an older child, explain that pornography includes pictures, videos, or written descriptions of sexual activity or nudity that is intended to elicit a sexual response. It can be found in magazines, movies, the Internet, books, photos, and video games.

Warn Kids about How Harmful It Is to Them Personally and to Those around Them

✦ It changes how our brain is wired, potentially leading to a full-blown addiction.

✦ It distorts our views of sex, and changes the way women are viewed.

✦ It hurts women and children by creating greater demand for sex trafficking.

✦ It emasculates many men, making them unable to be aroused and have a real-life sexual relationship. (This would be something you could cover with an older teen. He needs to know that it not only can affect him mentally but also physically.)

Give Kids an Action Plan to Reject Pornography

✦ Teach your kids to immediately look away and turn off the computer or device. (Pornographers often make it very difficult to exit a page you might stumble upon.)

✦ Encourage them to let you know (open communication is so important in preventing addiction).

✦ When they shut down a webpage, have them name it: "That was pornography."

✦ Teach them to distract themselves with something else (talking to someone, playing outside, prayer or devotional singing).

When we start having the conversation about pornography with our boys is important. Earlier rather than later is the recommendation. Kristen Jensen, author of *Good Pictures, Bad Pictures*, opened my eyes to how to have this conversation with even kids as young as five and arm them with an action plan so they are prepared to resist the allure of pornography. I read her book to my children and was surprised by how easy it was to open this conversation with them. I now recommend it to every parent I meet. Our kids need to know what pornography does to the brain and how it damages relationships. Our boys need to understand that the pornography industry is well aware of the addictive nature of its wares. Many experts are now saying that this kind of addiction is more powerful and harder to break than a cocaine habit.[8] Arming our children early with these facts and a plan for saying no prepares them for *when*

8. "Porn Changes the Brain," Fight the New Drug, August 18, 2014. Available at fightthenewdrug.org/porn-changes-the-brain.

they will inevitably encounter opportunities to view pornography.

And kids have ready access right at their fingertips. Gone
are the days of merely finding a boy with a *Playboy* magazine
stashed away. With a few clicks on a phone or tablet, they
have access to hardcore pornography that makes *Playboy*
look mild.

If we want to address the objectification of women in
our culture and help our boys embody the ideals of chivalric knighthood, we must talk to them about porn. I was ap-
prehensive about having this conversation, but there are
wonderful resources out there to help you along the way,
such as *Good Pictures, Bad Pictures*. Our boys need to
know that it is imperative to protect not only the dignity of
the women around them but their own dignity as well.

How do we teach our boys to value women as people and
not objects? Here is what it looks like in our home:

♦ We do not tolerate sexual innuendos and jokes.
♦ We do not use the term *sexy* or *hot* because those
terms focus exclusively on physical sexual appeal; instead we use terms such as *pretty* and *beautiful, lovely*
and *cute* to describe a girl or a woman.
♦ We have an open and honest dialogue about how to
have integrity in an anything-goes society.
♦ We discuss the dangers of pornography and give our
boys tools to protect themselves.
♦ We put Internet filters on all our devices (including
cellphones and tablets).

The stakes are high and our resolve is firm. We will raise boys, knights-in-the-making, who will grow up to become the husbands, fathers, and leaders of tomorrow. We realize that we can help them embrace a healthy and respectful view toward women today in their roles as brothers, sons, and friends by equipping them to say no to the lure of pornography.

✢ Creating an Atmosphere of Respect for Women

Creating an atmosphere of respect for women will have a powerful impact on your son for the rest of his life. To get you started, here are a few things to remember.

Just as a squire learned by following a knight's example, modern-day role models are needed within the family, the community, and the media our boys consume. Instruction is not enough; demonstration, both in reality and in narrative, is necessary to see this lived out practically. Boys need plenty of practice and affirmation so that they can discover and internalize what it means to be a strong man with a tender heart.

✢ It Starts at Home

The home provides the perfect context for modeling and teaching respect for women. It is the greenhouse in which a boy learns how to love, care for, and protect the women in his life. A knight always stands up for the women he loves—his mother, his sisters, his friends, and eventually, his wife. It is the place where he first learns to value women as people, and not as objects to be used for selfish gain, and to appreciate what makes women unique. Training starts early. A boy needs to know that it is never OK to hit a woman or to threaten her. He learns the importance of looking women (and people in general) straight in the eye, long before hormones cause him to want to look elsewhere. As he watches how a mother conducts herself, how a man treats his wife, how a couple interacts with each other, and how a boy is taught to treat his sister, he learns to traverse interactions with other women who will come into his life.

The home is the place where a mother can build up her son. When a woman shows admiration and respect for a man's strength, for his love, for his devotion, it builds him up. It motivates him to love and honor her in return. Love and respect goes both ways, and as mothers we do this when we acknowledge their gentlemanly conduct. We can encourage our daughters to recognize and admire when deeds of bravery and valor or just common courtesy are committed in their honor. They thank their brother when he offers to clear her dishes from the table. We admire him when he stops his silly antics so she can get a nice picture. We celebrate when he steps in to protect her by killing the invading insect. Boys want to be recognized and praised for their attempts. Of course, they do it for love, but they will do even more when recognized and honored.

On a Friday afternoon a few years ago, my husband

called to see how my day was going. Instantly, my mind was transported back to the morning. That moment when I just sat with my head in my hands, so frustrated. My boys had been disrespectful, and while the problem had been addressed, I was discouraged, I felt like throwing in the towel.

That evening, my husband resolutely walked in the garage door and called for our boys. And in that moment, I fell in love with him all over again.

He calmly, but firmly, told the boys that they were not allowed to treat his bride the way they had that morning. Because of their attitudes, there would be another consequence the following morning. Boys sat stiff, intently listening to Dad.

Bright and early, he took our boys and charged them with pulling all of the weeds in our infested front yard because dishonor had taken root in their hearts. Those boys, with tender fingers and tired bodies, learned a valuable lesson that day.

1. Respect and honor are important.
2. Disrespect will not be tolerated.
3. Don't mess with Mom or you deal with Dad.

Parenting is hard work and there are days when I just want to wave the little white flag and give up. But when that knight in shining armor rides up to my defense, I realize we are in this adventure together. What our children learn now extends far beyond what they receive in school. All of life provides lessons that will prepare them for the day they too will be given charge over a realm. It prepares them for the opportunities they have to step in and defend the honor of a woman.

✠ Find Additional Role Models

Fathers are not the only ones who can model to our boys what it means to be a man and how to interact respectfully with women. Our boys are watching all of the men around them as they formulate in their minds what it means to become a man and how to relate to girls and women. Uncles, grandfathers, a friend's dad, that teacher or coach can and will play a role in helping our boys develop healthy relationships with the women in their own lives.

We encourage our boys to look for friends who model this and to set an example themselves by challenging their friends in this area. When this happens they can change the entire culture of their community.

I was blessed to find such a community during my college years. I will never forget the football games we attended. A whole group of us snagged the first three rows on the fifty-yard line in the student section. At one particular game, I was standing in the back of our section with a friend. A guy behind me was drinking hard liquor he had sneaked into the facility, and in between taunting the players on the field, he aimed a few sexual slurs at the two of us. The withering look I gave him just seemed to goad him on and soon he was dipping the end of my braid into his liquor laced coke. Two guys in front of us took notice and casually mentioned trading places. These two guys took up a protective stance behind us and the harassing came to an end. With college guys getting a bad rap these days, my thoughts often go to those two and many whom I knew like them. These are the kind of men we want to raise.

We want our boys to embody the spirit of Sir Gareth of Orkney, the Kitchen Knight, to become men who know who they are, keep their cool no matter the circumstances, and always treat the women around them with respect.

Our boys have the opportunity to restore civility—especially in their relationships with the women in their lives. Training starts early and continues throughout their life as our young squires learn how to relate to the opposite sex and treat women with respect and honor, both because of the similarities they share as human beings and because of the glorious differences that make us stronger as a people.

✦ Throwing Down the Gauntlet

Challenge your boy to become a gentleman. Here are some ideas and discussion topics that will equip him to succeed in this iconic aspect of the Code of Chivalry by showing respect and honor to women with his words and by his actions. This takes practice, practice, practice!

✦ Talk about the similarities and differences between boys and girls, men and women.

◆ Who are the women in his life?

◆ Brainstorm together ways he can show honor and respect to women.

◆ Discuss why it is never, never OK to hit a woman, whether you are two, twenty, or eighty.

◆ Look people in the eye. The eyes are the window to the soul. Have your child practice looking you in the eye when you talk and to look others in the eye as well.

◆ Open doors for others. It is polite and a sign of respect to open a door for a lady. Challenge your son to be on the lookout as he goes through doors in public places to hold them open for someone else who is coming, especially if it is a woman.

◆ Let women, those with small children, or the elderly onto the elevator first. Even a boy of six or seven will take pride in allowing a mother with younger children get on first. (While this has nothing specifically to do with honoring women, it is courteous to allow those who are on the elevator to exit before you get on. Typically, this is something that also requires practice.)

◆ If you come to the door at the same time as a woman, you not only open the door for her, but you gesture for her to go through first, indicating your deference and protective care.

◆ Give up your seat. Whether it is a family gathering or a ride on public transportation, young squires look for opportunities to offer their seat to a lady.

◆ When walking with a lady, take the position of walking next to the street. (This is obviously not for a very young boy.)

◆ Look away, walk away. When your boy encounters situations in which a woman is degraded through pornography or provocative images, he should choose to look away and/or walk away.

CHAPTER 11

The Code: Don't Give Offense

✦ *Refrain from Wanton Offense*

A knight uses his strength only for good. He does not deliberately provoke a fight or seek to offend. To pick on someone is not a sign of bravery. A true knight realizes that his hands and his mouth can be used as both weapons and purveyors of peace.

WANTON IS AN old Saxon word that literally means "badly trained." It came to denote behavior indicating someone without breeding, someone left to his own devices on how to live, get along, and survive.

What does bullying and belching have to do with one another? They both constitute the wanton giving of offense. While the effects of the first might have a greater impact on others than the latter, they both boil down to a lack of care and consideration for others and a dearth of awareness and self-control. A true knight does not get distracted by the inconsequential and does not see a fight where there is none. He does not provoke. A knight in training learns to master his tongue and his fists instead of allowing them to master him.

Lack of basic manners is also a way of giving offense. Picking your nose, passing gas, belching, and other bodily responses have their time and place. While boys derive immense satisfaction from unleashing such "weapons," a true knight develops the situational awareness skills needed to determine when and where to not engage in such activities. He understands that there is a difference between how he conducts himself while eating dinner on a camping trip with his buddies versus eating dinner at a beautifully laid table alongside important guests. He understands that it is OK to run around boisterously at the park, but that he must conduct himself with quiet reserve at the library.

Our boys need careful, patient training just as much today as a page did in the Middle Ages. This duty must not be neglected because habits in these areas have an incredible impact not only on the lives of others but also on one's own life. It is the job of parents, primarily, but also other adults in a child's life to ensure that he gets this training, because most of it happens in the context of living life.

Kids fight, sometimes just for fun and sometimes for real. They tease, and occasionally it goes too far. They giggle and laugh while dribbling food all over the table. They will talk over others, interrupt you while you are trying to have a conversation with another adult, and will say something totally inappropriate at just the wrong time. Helping your kids in this area requires lots of work because children are not born civilized. It is our job to civilize them. Perseverance is essential; the payoff incalculable.

So here are some practical areas to work on good behavior with our boys.

✛ Learning to Listen and Watch for Clues

"Do not provoke" is a common refrain heard in our home. Children, boys especially, are not born with this kind of social awareness. Boys love to tease and roughhouse, but it is imperative that we teach them the difference between doing it in fun and recognizing when it slips over into the realm of harassment. Sometimes this requires us to get down at their level and ask questions to help them develop empathy and learn how to listen or watch for objections. There were many times when I would hear myself asking, "When your brother (or sister) said 'Please stop,' what do you think he meant?"

Circling back to Sir Gareth and his experience in King Arthur's court gives us an excellent opportunity to talk about what it means to refrain from the wanton giving of offense. According to legend, King Arthur was amused and intrigued by Gareth's mysterious request for food and lodging before he would reveal his identity and purpose for coming to the king's court. Arthur ordered that every courtesy be given to this mystery man. Sir Kay, who was charged with the care of the new guest, judged him to be a commoner merely looking for a handout. Ignoring Arthur's directive, Sir Kay took up an offense that was not there. Kay's scorn was so severe that he proceeded to taunt Gareth for the next year, relegated him to the servants' quarters, and ordered him to work in the kitchen. Mortified by this rude behavior, Sir Lancelot offered to intervene, but Gareth chose to deal with his situation without complaint.

This narrative provides a sharp contrast in the character of these knights. Sir Kay was stingy and rude. He took offense and then tried to provoke Gareth. While a strong and loyal knight, his volatile and cruel nature marred his reputation. He created conflict where there should have been none. Lancelot treated this mystery man with kindness, demonstrating his true greatness as a man.

In our home, we have seen similar scenarios where either a boy will badger someone else over a perceived offense that is not his problem (as in Kay's example) or outright provoke another for no reason at all.

Our young men need to be reminded to not get distracted by the inconsequential, as Sir Kay was. Or as Abraham Lincoln once said, "We should be too big to take offense and too noble to give it." We need to challenge our boys and to challenge ourselves to focus on what matters. Whenever possible, we need to seek to live at peace with those around us and purposefully overlook offenses.

We give our boys the same advice that Geoffroi de Charny gave to the knights of his time:

Above all, avoid quarrels, for a quarrel with one's equal is dangerous, a quarrel with someone higher in rank is madness, and a quarrel with someone lower in rank is a vile thing, but a quarrel with a fool or a drunk is an even viler thing.[1]

✠ Controlling the Tongue

The old saying goes "Sticks and stones may break my bones, but words will never hurt me." Except that they do. Words wield power and cannot be retracted. Once spoken they hang in the air and in our minds.

As we pored over pictures of knights and their armor, I drew my boys' attention to the helmets and encouraged them to imagine that the visor that covers the face could offer two-way protection. Not only does it protect weapons from getting in but it can remind the knight to not unleash his verbal weapons. Once those words are hurled beyond the confines of the helmet, they cannot be retracted. We need to think before we speak and heed the old proverb, "He who guards his mouth and his tongue, guards his soul from troubles."[2]

---

1. Geoffroi de Charny, *A Knight's Own Book of Chivalry* (Philadelphia: University of Pennsylvania Press, 2005), p. 71.
2. Proverbs 21:23, New American Standard Version.

✝ When a Boy Discovers His Hands

"I see you've discovered your hands, son," my friend said as he sat down to talk with his boy. Earlier that day, his six-year-old had randomly punched another boy in that place where no one should ever kick or punch.

"Why did you do that?"

"I dunno."

"Do you remember when we played catch last year and a ball hit you there?"

"Yes . . ." the boy responded, cringing and inadvertently recoiling at the memory.

My friend proceeded to explain how serious his son's actions had been. Like any other weapon, one needs to be very careful about when and how to use them. Just like this dad did, we need to teach our boys that while there might be an occasional need to use their fists to protect someone or for self-defense, they are never to be used offensively and never unprovoked.

It is important to make this distinction clear. One of those instances came up in the news as a new school year started in 2015. Seventeen-year-old Cody Pines, a senior at Huntington Beach High School, was walking along when he saw an altercation begin. A boy repeatedly started striking an acquaintance of Cody's, a boy who was legally blind. Cody ran to intervene, landing one powerful punch that floored the instigator.

That one punch saved his friend from countless more.

While Cody could have run for help, his quick intervention stopped the aggression in its tracks. There is a time and a place to use your fist, and this was one of them.

✝ Learning the Art of Disagreeing

Talking to our children about not provoking one another, either in word or deed, provides the perfect opportunity to discuss the art of disagreeing. We refer, yet again, to Abraham Lincoln: "Do I not destroy my enemies when I make them my friends?"

In the midst of the bickering and the fighting and when our boys take on the role of a bully, we need to help them find solutions. We need to teach our sons how to communicate their thoughts and feelings in a productive manner that wins people over or, at the very least, causes them to hear you out rather than offending them from the get-go. We want our boys to pursue winsome over wanton.

✝ Manners Matter

> *Whoso will of courtesy hear,*
> *In this book it is all made clear;*
> *If thou be gentleman, yeoman, or knave,*
> *Thee needeth nurture for to have.*

These lines come from a poem contained in *The Babees Book*, which, despite its infantile title, all pages and squires studied. This book outlined an elaborate system of rules and etiquette that had developed in medieval Europe to guide interactions between people. Learning manners and etiquette was critical for keeping peace.

Because of its centrality in social life, mealtime garnered special focus. It was common for two people to share a trencher at meals. This trencher, a large stale piece of bread, stood in for a plate and bowl. Each person would get a spoon and everyone carried a personal knife to use at meals, but the trencher was shared. As such it was vital to learn how to take turns and share. Everyone would wash their hands and remove the dirt from under their fingernails before entering the banquet room. Failing to do so was the height of rudeness.

Eating together was a communal event, it was the time to share tales of adventure and news from the community or distant lands. A page learned the rules of courtesy during mealtime through study of these books and on-the-job training while serving.

What is considered proper manners changes over time and across cultures. What may have been proper etiquette in the Middle Ages, such as backing out of a room after addressing their lord or eating after all of the adults have had their fill, are now antiquated by today's standards. But the principles still remain: Do not offend. We have the opportunity in our everyday lives to teach our boys to be perceptive and attentive to etiquette in different situations out of courtesy toward others. Having a mind-set that pursues courtesy will serve our boys well no matter what they do or where they go in life.

✦ One Must Know the Rules to Play Well

Panic and frustration was setting in, as I second-guessed my decision to brave the library with my three young boys. First, they fought over a book before almost mowing down a little old lady. The final straw came when they yelled for me from across the room because I turned around for a moment to try to secure a few books to check out. Don't they know about library voices?

My voice terse, I scooped up the eighteen-month-old at my feet and gave my other two the evil eye and said, "We're leaving now." I stewed on the way home, embarrassed at their obnoxious behavior and vowing to never again darken the doors of a library until they were at least twenty.

Time has a way of bringing perspective, and I realized that I had never formally taught them how to behave in the library. As frustrated as I was that they were not playing by the rules, they were frustrated too. No one likes to get the evil eye from Mom, especially if you cannot figure out why.

Full of resolve the next week, I dutifully set out for the library. At the entrance I gathered my little team around and shared with them the rules for the library game. They were to use inside voices, demonstration required. Running was not allowed. To get my attention, they were to come over, touch my arm, and whisper in my ear. Fighting was strictly prohibited. "Do you understand the rules for winning at the library?" I asked my sports-minded little boys. *"Yes!!!"* they cheered, before switching to a silent cheer and high fives.

It is unfair to get upset when we take our kids into situations for which we have not clearly communicated expectations. Despite bumps along this road, that day was a turning point. We now lay out expectations before we go anyplace new. They appreciate knowing how to behave because life is better when the rules of courtesy are clearly understood.

✚ Nudge, Don't Nag

While laying out expectations is important, it is equally important to take care how we follow up on their training. Children need reminders. It is unfair and unrealistic to expect them to instantly take up new habits with absolute perfection.

We need to nudge, but not nag. The difference lies in tone. Giving calm, cheerful reminders of the right way to do things is far easier to accept than biting criticism of what they are doing wrong. They will make more progress and your home will be a more peaceful place if you can stick to the first approach.

Everyone benefits from this, no matter what sex, age, or struggles in life. Dr. Temple Grandin, a world-renowned autism spokeswoman, recalls with fondness the training she received in manners as a girl in the 1950s. She explains that with proper instruction, *anyone* can develop good manners:

> When mistakes were made, I was given proper instructions instead of mother or a neighbor saying "No." If I wiped my mouth with my hand, my mother would say, "Use the napkin." The mistake made by many parents and teachers is to say "no" instead of giving the instruction. When I twirled my fork around my head she would say, "Put it back on your plate."[3]

We too should teach manners and courtesy in a calm, neutral tone. Although the message is the same, the way it is communicated makes all the difference in the world.

✦ Cultivating the Seeds of Courtesy

As in the Middle Ages, the most powerful place to inculcate these lessons on interpersonal skills is at home, specifically at the dinner table. Slowing down to savor food and conversation connects us relationally, gives us a peek into the souls of others, and provides the perfect opportunity to cultivate the seeds of courtesy.

3. Temple Grandin, "The Way I See It: Using 1950's Parenting Methods," Autism Asperger's Digest. Available at autismdigest.com/the-way-i-see-it-using-1950s -parenting-methods.

At the dinner table, children learn how to converse and how to relate in society. We must not allow mealtimes to be rushed or full of strife. In this hectic age, it requires making a conscious effort to reclaim this opportunity to spend quality time together.

Clearly communicate ground rules. For instance, the family meal should be a conflict-free zone. There is a time and place to bring complaints up; the dinner table is not one of those places. That starts with parents and trickles down to kids.

Most lessons about polite conversation will happen in the moment as boys learn about appropriate and inappropriate dinnertime discussions. Learning the seemingly dying art of having a conversation is invaluable. Our young pages will learn not only appropriate topics but how to listen, how to ask questions, and how to respond to a topic, rather than changing it. Studies show that more frequent family dinners are related to fewer behavioral problems, greater emotional well-being, more trusting and helpful behaviors toward others, and higher life satisfaction.[4]

In addition to the dinner table, we prepare our sons in our homes for all other interpersonal interactions. They practice handshakes with grandparents. We host an occasional party during which they learn how to greet one an-

---

4. Elgar FJ, Craig W, Trites SJ, "Family Dinners, Communication, and Mental Health in Canadian Adolescents," *Journal of Adolescent Health* 52, no. 4 (2013): 433–38.

other and extend hospitality. We practice fancy manners at home before taking them to a nice restaurant or event. They join us for meals with other adults where they have the opportunity to watch and listen and learn.

✤ Situational Awareness

Good manners boil down to being aware of others, not memorizing a bunch of rules. Just as we help our children build situational awareness skills to stand against injustice or protect the weak, we talk to them about the importance of this kind of awareness in extending courtesy.

Context is important. Belching in the backyard with your buddies is OK. Belching at the dinner table is not. We play tag at the park but not at church. We sing silly songs in the car but not on an airplane. We are preparing them to read their environment and have the situational awareness and self-control to behave appropriately in each situation.

Theodore Roosevelt said, "Courtesy is as much a mark of a gentleman as courage." Learning the art of not giving offense takes practice. It is of utmost importance to not neglect this aspect of their training. In this area, we often use the excuse that boys will be boys. A boy can and ought to learn how to become a man of worth and respect. This will open doors for him that even the best education cannot. Creating a habit of putting others first is a win for everyone.

Whether careless or deliberate, offending behavior is not becoming of a true knight. Let's raise boys who are marked for their sensibility, awareness, discernment, and acumen—boys who are well practiced in the art of not giving wanton offense.

✣ Throwing Down the Gauntlet

Here are some ideas to get you going on teaching your boys to not give offense. Feel free to modify the suggestions to fit your own cultural context.

Learning to Live at Peace with Others

- ✦ Teach your kids to ask themselves, "Is this worth fighting about?" If so, what would be the best way to proceed?
- ✦ Help them find a way to calm down before talking about a problem. I taught one of my toddlers to start clapping when he felt like hitting. Older boys may need to learn to walk away and cool down before working through a problem with someone.
- ✦ Practice making faces or role-playing various emotions (using full body language) so your kids will be better equipped to recognize the needs of others and not wantonly give offense.

General Manners

✦ Make sure your boys say please, thank you, excuse me, pardon me. (They really are magic words that provide an excellent foundation in not giving offense.)

✦ Continue to work on honorifics (see Chapter 7).

✦ Establish and review your family rules. Here are some examples:

 ▪ Potty humor belongs in the bathroom.

 ▪ Gross noises can be made outdoors or in your room, but not in the company of ladies or in public places.

 ▪ Passing gas belongs in the bathroom. If some escapes in front of others own it like a man and say, "Excuse me."

 ▪ Keep your mouth closed and/or cover your mouth, if you feel a burp coming that you cannot stop.

Greeting Others

✦ Get in the habit of saying good morning, good afternoon, and good evening.

✦ Practice greeting someone: firm handshake, look the person in the eye, say something, such as hello, nice to meet you, my name is ___.

✦ Practice introducing people by saying, "Hi ___, I'd like you to meet my friend ___." "Mrs. Smith, have you met my brother ___?"

Practice Table Manners

Add and focus on developing a couple of habits at a time. Boys will be overwhelmed and frustrated if you try to tackle many new guidelines at once. Some manners are most fitting for more formal occasions, but kids need to know how to behave *before* they find themselves in those situations.

Table Manners

✦ Knights in training learn to:

- Say grace. No eating until this happens.
- Place their napkin in their lap at the beginning of each meal.
- Hold a fork properly.
- Get food from the fork to their mouth correctly.
- Cut food properly.
- Use their knife (not their fingers) to scoot food onto a fork.
- Keep their nondominant hand in their lap when not needed.
- Chew quietly and politely without smacking lips and with their mouths closed.
- Not talk with their mouth full. (Put a finger up to indicate that you need to swallow first.)
- Keep their elbows off the table until they are done

eating or, according to *The Babees Book*, "Look ye be not caught leaning on the table." (In military academies, a cadet used to have to eat while keeping his elbows glued to his side, so he would not jostle those next to him. Try eating military style.)

- Thank Mom, or whoever made the meal, for a nice dinner. Young squires should also find one or two nice things to say about the meal, even if they did not like everything. (Parents may need to help them the first few times.)
- Ask to be excused.
- Clear their plate, utensils, and napkin from the table.

✦ Young squires are taught that if they are eating at a friend's house, they eat what is offered. It is wise to train even little ones to take a few bites of whatever is served.

✦ Try having your boys eat a meal (or several) with a mirror in front of them so they can see what good manners or poor manners look like.

✦ Have your boys practice eating a fancy meal as if important dignitaries from around the world were at the table. Pull out the best dishes, use all of the forks, knives, and spoons. Continue to practice this skill a couple of times a year. Holidays can be the perfect time to enjoy this kind of fine dining.

Communicate Etiquette and Expectations in Different Situations

✦ Do not expect children to behave if you have not clearly laid out expectations. Before you go to a place where you expect certain behavior, take time to review the rules of etiquette.

✦ When at the library, at church, or other quiet places, our boys should learn to:

- Use inside voices.
- Refrain from running.
- Let Mom know where they are.
- Remove their hat.

✦ When young squires accompany you to the grocery store they know to:

- Avoid running.
- Stay next to the cart.
- Not whine.
- Ask politely for something, but recognize that no means no. (See previous point.)
- Help mom put groceries on conveyer belt.
- Help load groceries into the car and then into the house.

✦ When at school or in a classroom, knights in training:

- Give the teacher their full attention.
- Do not talk to their friends while someone else is speaking.
- Do not interrupt the teacher, but raise their hand and wait to be called on.
- Do not run or goof off.

✦ When visiting a friend, our boys should:

- "Not rush in rudely, but enter with head up and at an easy pace," as it says in *The Babees Book*. Greet everyone, but especially the adults in the home before running off to play.
- Ask if they need to take their shoes off.
- Abide by house rules, even if they differ from their rules at home.
- Offer to help tidy up at the end.

■ Thank the adult of the home as well as their friend for having them over.

Situational Awareness

✦ Play a game called "is this appropriate?" by reviewing when and where certain behaviors are allowed. Here are some suggestions:

■ **Belching/burping.** Outside with your buddies, not at the dinner table or in the company of others. Cover your mouth and say "Excuse me" afterward if one slips out.

■ **Sneezing/coughing.** Into your elbow and always turn away from people or food. Say "Excuse me" afterward.

■ **Blowing your nose.** Step away from others to blow your nose.

■ **Picking your nose.** Go to the bathroom!

■ **Passing gas.** This may be funny with your close friends, but it is awkward any other time. Get thee to a bathroom.

■ **Teasing.** This is a tricky one. It can be done in small doses in jest if the other person approves. Watch for signs that the other person wants you to stop and then *stop*.

■ **Loud, boisterous cheering.** Loud cheering at a football game or basketball game is encouraged, but not on the golf course.

Medieval Roots of Present-Day Manners

✦ **Salute.** *Comes from knights who would raise their visor to signify that they did not mean to fight.*

✦ **Raising a hat to a lady.** *Also sprang from this knightly tradition of lifting the visor to signify peace.*

✦ **Shaking with the right hand.** *Offering an empty right hand signified that a knight came in peace.*

✦ **Removing your hat indoors.** *A man putting down his walking stick and removing his hat dates back to when a knight would leave his sword and helmet at the door.*

+ CHAPTER 12

The Code: Speak Truth

+ Speak the Truth at All Times

A brave knight is a man of both physical strength and strength of mind and heart. He tells the truth at all times, even if it means acknowledging that he has done wrong or made a mistake.

GROGGY AND A LITTLE DISORIENTED, six-year-old William Marshal was delivered to the camp of King Stephen. His father had promised to surrender Newberry Castle to the king, and the boy was taken from his family home in the night as a surety for his father's pledge. Soon scouts arrived to report that William's father, John Marshal, had sneaked food and more soldiers into the castle under cover of darkness. He had no intention of surrendering, no intention of keeping his promises.

Providentially, young William survived this encounter. While the deal had been the castle for the boy's life, King Stephen could not go through with killing the young boy. This defining moment in William's life could have set him on the road to despair, but he was destined to chart a course far different from his father's, as he overcame abandonment and became one of the greatest knights of all time—brave and true. He would be a knight known for his integrity and one who rose from the obscurity of being the discarded younger son to deftly defending and serving under five different English kings.

This was a man keenly affected by a broken pledge and yet one who was determined to be known as a man of his word, a truth teller.

✛ A Knight's Honor: Honesty

As defenders of all that is right and good, it was of utmost importance that a knight have a reputation of being trustworthy. Lying either to protect himself or to get something he wanted was the antithesis of knighthood because a true knight would not put his own needs and desires above another's. It is vital that our boys understand the importance and value of speaking the truth, that it is the right and honorable thing to do. When a knight—a man of honor—makes a mistake, he owns up to it. It can be challenging, but he does not hide behind excuses or spread falsehoods. He is brave enough to come clean and face the consequences, knowing that he will be the better for it. A knight who speaks falsehood is not trusted with responsibility and is not shown honor. There is safety in the presence of a trustworthy man, and he is given more responsibility and respect because of this trustworthiness.

Three hundred years before William Marshal lived, Dhuoda, a noblewoman from the ninth century, gave us a peek into the values and ethics a mother sought to pass on to her boy, in a book of instructions she wrote and sent to her son, also named William, after he left for the emperor's court. She admonishes her son that a man of strength walks without blemish—choosing not to sin when it would be easy to do so. He works justice and speaks truthfully, without deceit.[1]

She writes, "Be truthful to your lord, my son William. Be vigilant, energetic, and offer him ready assistance." She continues, "The eloquence of a great man is therefore a favor greater than silver and gold because his lips draw from the honeycomb and his words are pure words . . . tried by the fire, purged."[2]

---

1. Clella I. Jaffe, "Ethics in the Family: A Ninth Century Mother Trains Her Sons," *EJC\REC* 7, no.1 (1997). Available at cios.org/EJCPUBLIC/007/1/00715.HTML.
2. Dhuoda, *Handbook for William: A Carolingian Woman's Counsel to her Son, 841 AD*, trans. [Carol Neel] (Washington, D.C: The Catholic University of America Press, 1999), p. 27.

✟ Knight or Knave, You Decide

When it comes to throwing down the gauntlet and challenging our children to pursue honesty, the choice is simple: Knight or knave, you decide. Our boys can train to become knights or practice the pursuit of knavery.

Although the term *knave* originally denoted a boy or male servant, during the Middle Ages it morphed into a description of a person's character. A knave is a tricky, deceitful fellow. His reputation follows him everywhere, and no one trusts him. What is worse, he cannot trust anyone else either. He lacks something that most people crave—respect from those around him.

In their words and by their actions our boys have the opportunity each and every day to take on the identity of a knight or a knave. With this chivalry challenge we encourage our boys to pursue the worthy habit of truth telling.

Inspiring our kids toward an ideal is far more profound and effective than threatening them merely with punishment for transgressions. Although there should be consequences for lying, we need to inspire and equip them to pursue truth. Dr. Victoria Talwar and her team at McGill Hill University discovered that children were more apt to tell the truth when given a moral reason to do so and when truthfulness was the expectation.[3] This proved far more ef-

---

3. V. Talwar, C. Arruda, and S. Yachison "The Effects of Punishment and Appeals for Honesty on Children's Truth-Telling Behavior," *Journal of Experimental Child Psychology* 130 (2014): 209–17.

fective than simply informing children about the consequences of lying.

A knight who speaks the truth and is honest in his dealings with others garners respect. He has the ear of kings and those in authority over him. He is sent on the most exciting and daring quests because he is dependable.

This chivalry challenge affords opportunity to talk about the principles of honesty and equip our children to navigate through the challenges of everyday life in honest ways. Talwar recommends giving them reasons to be honest, but then in response to a lie to be firm and serious, saying something like, "That sounds like you're not telling the truth" or "Are you absolutely sure that's what happened?"

What follows are some of the *whys* we can discuss with our sons as well as a few *caveats* for situations when telling the absolute, unguarded truth may not be the best policy.

✠ Why Should We Tell the Truth?

Telling the truth is the right thing to do. Cultures all over the world and all across time value honesty. Telling the truth feels good. You know you are a person of integrity.

Telling the truth is a sign of strength. Telling the truth takes guts; it reveals you are brave. The time will come when our boys will need to speak truth when confronting a friend about a dangerous situation or when a friend is making a wrong decision. It might mean having to tell a trusted adult the truth or risk offending a friend. Telling the truth can also be hard because there are real consequences not only for bad things we do but also for mistakes we make. I will never forget the time one of our boys owned up to throwing the first punch in a brother brawl after we had discussed this knightly principle even though it meant facing a predetermined consequence for that kind of action.

Telling the truth builds trust in relationships. Trust and respect are essential for healthy relationships, not only among family and friends but from everyone. When you have a reputation for honesty, you are trusted by parents, other leaders, and your peers.

Telling the truth is freeing. It is stressful to live trapped in the midst of lies. There is freedom when we come clean and tell the truth. Speaking truth allows one to walk free from the effects of this kind of stress.

✚ Why Do We Lie?

When talking about honesty with our children, it helps to get to the root cause for why they are speaking dishonestly in that moment. Their reasoning helps us as parents determine how to deal with each situation. Lying can become a go-to solution because children lack problem-solving skills to navigate tricky situations.[4] It is important to look for ways to equip our children.

Here are a few reasons they might lie:

From a lack of understanding between reality and fantasy for younger children.

Out of fear or shame and/or the belief they will be punished and not be accepted.

Out of selfishness or spite, usually to protect themselves or to get something they want.

To protect someone's feelings.

There are developmental aspects to consider when our children are in the four- to six-year-old range. This is the age of imaginary friends, talking animals, and horned monsters. One of my boys had a friend, Peter, who went everywhere with him. In addition, there are times at this age when our children do not intend to deceive but rather communicate what they wish were true. These are communication deficits rather than deception issues. The child is declaring his wished reality. Instead of accusing him of

---

4. Janet Lehman, "How to Deal with Lying in Children and Teens," *Empowering Parents*. Available at empoweringparents.com/article/how-to-deal-with-lying-in -children-and-teens.

lying, help your young one start to distinguish between fantasy and reality.

A little boy may announce that his parents are going to take him out for ice cream. While this is not true, he certainly wishes it were true. Helping him understand and communicate his desires improves his ability to discern wishes from reality and gives him a way to communicate those wishes accurately.

Recently I asked my four-year-old to put away her shoes. The shoes made it to the door of her bedroom before something else distracted her attention. When I found them and told her she needed to finish what I had asked her to do, she responded with, "I tried." She had not tried, but instead of pointing this out I asked if she meant that she would try next time. She nodded. I had her repeat the accurate statement back to me before she picked up her shoes and finished putting them away.

To help our young children build a habit of honesty sometimes it is better to simply state the truth.

I try to remember this, but sometimes forget. It only took one step into my four-year-old's room a while back to realize I had a load of sheets to do. For some reason, I felt compelled to ask the obvious, "Did you wet the bed, honey?" She must have sensed the resignation in my voice at the thought of an extra load of laundry because she vehemently denied it. Young kids want to feel safe and are just beginning to understand what it means to disappoint someone. Instead of accusing our children of lying at this age, it is better to avoid the confrontation in the first place simply by stating the truth. "I see you had an accident last night. Please help Mommy by bringing me your wet pj's and underwear." If you made the mistake of asking like I did, you need to acknowledge that you know the truth and help them to speak truth too. In this scenario, I said something like, "Accidents happen. It's OK. Let's get this cleaned up."

But what about those times when they lie out of willful self-preservation or out of spite? If we catch our child in a lie, knowing the root cause for it helps inform our response. Just as there are real consequences for adults who lie, there need to be consequences for our children. Privileges accompany trust. When trust is broken between a parent and child, their freedoms are restricted.

As they get older, you can discuss the consequences of lying that others face. The news is full of such examples. In the area of sports alone, your boys will see scenarios play out over and over again where an athlete is caught in lies and sometimes banned from the sports they play. It is important for our boys to see that there are real-life consequences for lying that affect us all.

✦ Using Tact to Temper Our Words

There is a needed caveat to this emphasis on the moral value of telling the truth. We need to make sure our words are both useful and kind as well as true. This is not the same as saying it is OK to lie. Instead, there are ways to express truth kindly and tactfully so as to protect the feelings of others. Not everything that goes through your head should come out of your mouth.

Children are not born with an inherent sense of tact. We need to explain that there are times when we do not divulge every detail about everything. For example, it is inappropriate to discuss the roadkill you saw in intimate detail at the dinner table when asked about your day. It is inappropriate for a child to tell someone who wants to talk to their parent that he or she is "going to pee" or even "in the restroom."

We have opportunities, almost daily, to teach our children to recognize when truth needs to be mixed with tact.

We teach our children to stop themselves before they speak and ask a couple of questions:

1. Is this useful?
2. Is this kind?

Learning this requires help from parents, but the payoff in the long run is invaluable.

✝ Do Not Be Ruled by Big Feelings

Emotional honesty is another challenging problem. I still remember a time when my emotions welled as a child. "I hate you." I screamed at my mother. I am not sure what reaction I was hoping to receive, probably contrition and acquiescing to my demands. I will never forget her response.

"You don't hate me, Heather."

"Yes, I do." I muttered almost under my breath.

"You don't hate me, you dislike my decision." She paused to let this sink in before calmly continuing.

Then she had me repeat back to her, "I don't hate you, I dislike that you won't take me to the park to see all of my friends."

This was a scenario that would play itself out several times until I finally internalized it and started to do it automatically. Kids (and adults too) have big feelings. It is important to acknowledge those and speak honestly about them. In the heat of the moment, I did not actually hate my mom. I was just really, really angry. She helped me home in on what I was feeling and react in both an honest and more productive manner. It is a lesson I have passed on to my own children. When they learn how to be honest with themselves, it is easier to be honest with others. Helping our children be honest with their feelings provides them a better opportunity to navigate conflict.

✠ Tall Tales Are Not Truth Claims

We love a good tall tale over here. Ever since we watched the old Davy Crockett movie, my boys have been obsessed with them. But we emphasize the thrill of spinning a yarn while explaining the importance of not using them to deceive.

Parenting expert and author Dr. Scott Turansky recommends having your children use cues to identify anything other than reality such as: "I think it happened this way." "I think this is the answer." "I'm not sure . . ." "Maybe . . ." (possibility) "I wish this were true." "I'd like it if . . ." (wish) "I'd like to tell you a story . . ." "I can imagine what it would be like to . . ." (fantasy)[5]

These cues have helped our family be clear in our communication. There is a time and place for both, and we weave tall tales when we are playing a game that calls for bluffing, pulling a silly prank, or entertaining each other with a good story.

✢ Weaving Webs and Forming Habits

One day as we were shooting hoops, I asked my boys how one can become a better basketball player. "Practice," they told me. The same goes for any skill, especially becoming a man of your word, I explained. The seeds of knighthood or knavery are cultivated by the habits of our everyday lives. How you practice determines how you will play when it counts. Whoever walks in integrity walks securely, but the one who makes his way crooked will always be found out.

Speaking the truth gets easier the more you do it. The same is true for lying. Once you start down the path of telling lies, they come out without even thinking about it. As Sir Walter Scott perceptively said, "Oh what a tangled web we weave when first we practice to deceive."

"Does anybody want to play a spiderweb game?" I called

5. Scott Turkansky, "10 Ways to Get Your Kids to Stop Lying," iMom. Available at imom.com/10-ways-to-get-your-kids-to-stop-lying.

out one day. The boys were immediately curious to see what the painter's tape and beanbags in my hand had to do with spiders and followed me over to the hallway. Gathering them around, I asked them if they could tell me a little bit about lies and truth telling.

"What does this have to do with spiders?" my middle one interjected.

"That's a fair question. Why does a spider spin a web?" The boys explained that spiderwebs are sticky and meant to catch bugs.

"Right! When we say something that is untrue it is like weaving a web, except that unlike spiders, we can get caught up in our own web of lies. The more we lie, the trickier it gets to navigate through life and eventually we get caught in that sticky web of our own making."

"Race to the end of the hallway and bring me that beanbag." I said, coming back to our game. Eagerly they complied. Afterward, I put up a couple of sticky web strands of painter's tape in the hallway and challenged them to the same beanbag retrieval race.

As they caught their breath I explained that many times we do not stop at just one lie, but end up telling more to cover for the others. It can become a habit that makes life even trickier because you must remember all of your lies to keep up your story. We then circled back to talking about lies and why we tell them.

They continued to race as lies continued to be added. Soon they were ducking, jumping, and crawling—completely forgetting why they even started this game in the first place.

Eventually one of the boys was caught. Tears ensued, and we sat down to talk about it. They all agreed that it would not be pleasant to live life sneaking around. "What would you think if I told you there was a way to clear the web away?" They were all ears at this point as I explained that the only way to defeat a web of lies is to come clean and tell the truth. When we tell the truth, we get to clear the web. It is still a messy job, but it is the only way to rebuild trust and walk in freedom again.

Freedom. Now that is a beautiful path to walk and one we can point our boys toward when we establish a home where honesty is valued and create a safe haven that welcomes confession. This does not mean you remove consequences. But it involves clearly and frequently communicating that your love for your children does not hinge on their behavior. It involves communicating that you both are on the same team and you want to prepare them to be brave, and strong, and *true*.

We did not end our little game with the bad news of having to tiptoe around lies and eventually getting caught. Bringing our boys full circle into an awareness of the freedom that comes with clearing the air is powerful. Honesty leads to respect, especially when we fess up to mistakes or prior lies we have told. There is pain, but it is the only path to healing. There is freedom and dignity in pursuing honesty. It is only through fessing up to your fibs that you can begin to rebuild a habit of honesty that not only helps you but builds trust with those around you.

Our kids will make mistakes and they will willfully do

things that are wrong. It is human nature. Understanding this aspect about humanity helps us not overreact when they do confess something. They need to know that we love them regardless of their behavior and when they do take that step to come clean it is important that we do not over-react.

We have the opportunity to cast a vision for true and honest living. We can encourage our boys to establish good habits that will serve them well for the rest of their lives. Becoming a truth teller is a process. It takes courage to speak truth. But the truth sets us free.

✦ Throwing Down the Gauntlet

Ask your kids why people might lie. Talk about the four reasons people lie.

> From a lack of understanding between reality and fantasy for younger children.
> Out of fear or shame and/or the belief they will be punished or not be accepted.
> Out of selfishness or spite, usually to protect them-selves or to get something they want.
> To protect someone's feelings.

Clarify. Help your kids determine if what they are say-ing is true or something they want to be true. Help them practice ways to communicate while still remaining truthful.

> I wish versus I want versus This is what happened.
> *I hate you* really means "I don't like you right now because ___."

Tact and truthfulness. Talk about what to say when too much truth is not best.

> Receiving a gift you do not like. Instead of lying and saying you love it or being brutally honest and saying you hate it, find something true to say: "Wow, Grandma, thanks for thinking of me." "I can tell you put a lot of thought into this."
> If someone asks for your parent, instead of saying, "She is in the bathroom," or "She isn't here," say "She is unavailable at the moment."

Put on a reminder. Sometimes we need a visual reminder to speak truth. According to one medieval legend, a knight who was caught in a lie forever wore the magic belt he had lied about as a reminder to not go down that path again. Have your young page wear some kind of reminder, such as a rubber band or leather bracelet or ring as a reminder to be brave and true. Challenge him to ask himself the following questions before he speaks: Is this useful? Is this kind?

The game that never ends. Play go-fish with your child. Play a round or two in which everyone lies. What happens when everyone lies? (Answer: The game never ends.) Talk about the importance of truthfulness when playing games and in life.

Web of lies race. Gather painter's tape, a timer, and a piece of paper. Have your boys define what a lie is and explain that every time we lie, we send out a web around us. And why do spiders weave webs?

Clear the web. Challenge your young knights in training to clear the spiderwebs. If they are living a lie, encourage them to find freedom in tearing down the spiderwebs and confessing their lie to you. (Brace yourselves to not freak out but to react in a way that will help your child conquer whatever issue he has been trying to cover up. Remind yourself that you both are on the same team. Raising kids who are prepared for adulthood is far better than a hit to your reputation.)

Truth race. Go out and collect some rocks. Have your boys run a race with an empty backpack and then with a backpack that contains rocks. Ask your children which way of racing they preferred. Life is better when you can run without the burden of lies. The truth sets us free.

Live out honesty. Talk to your boys about situations in which honesty is important. Here are a few you could discuss:

Admitting you broke something.

Staying true to your word by following the rules.

Doing what you say you would do as soon as you are able or expected to.

Pay for items you want.

Return excess change.

Doing your own work instead of copying.

Discuss plagiarism. Plagiarism is a form of academic dishonesty. With an older child, discuss the importance of doing his own work. Talk to him about how to research and then put those ideas and information into his own words. Talk to him about the importance of not copying answers from others.

CHAPTER 13

The Code: Be Generous

> **✝ *Be Generous and Willing to Share***
>
> A great knight considers others more important than himself and is thus generous and willing to share what he has with friends and those in need.

"GEORGE, GEORGE, GEORGE!" The chants rose as the people realized he had vanquished the dragon. In gratitude they flooded out from the protection of the brass tower, showering him with gifts and praise.

According to the story of Saint George and the Dragon, the king and queen emerged, bestowing gifts of gold and jewels for the amazing feat he performed to rescue the kingdom. But in humility and generosity, George turned around and gave the money to the poor in the community, causing the rejoicing to swell to new heights. In return for his generosity, the king gave George his kingdom and consent to marry his daughter, whom the young knight had come to know.

It is a beautiful ending to an intense story and reveals many of the ideals of that time surrounding the importance of generosity. Whereas it is easy to be generous when someone has done something for you, and we should be, it is a truly big-hearted move to give back when nothing is expected.

Generosity was a highly prized virtue in medieval culture. Many a medieval tale starts out with a visitor warmly welcomed into the home, whether the castle of a noble or the humble cottage of a hermit. It was customary to open up one's home to others. A knight who possessed land would welcome others to stay with him in his castle. Often the household would prepare a feast in honor of their visitors. The host would be generous with his attention and time and in provision of food and shelter.

Generosity extended into the realms of charity. Charlemagne threw down the gauntlet to his own sons and nobles to be mindful of those in need. He urged a habit of charity that gave liberally to orphans and widows. We see this reflected in the thoughts of the ninth-century noblewoman Dhuoda, when she wrote a moving handbook of sorts to her son, who had left to serve in the court of the king. She instructed, "You must not fail to have pity for the poor, my son, for God often hears their voices . . . In fraternal compassion—for those who thirst, hunger, and are naked, to orphans and pilgrims, strangers and widows, and to little children and all the needy and oppressed—help them kindly, taking pity upon them whenever you see them."[1]

Greed and selfishness clouded one's character and branded one as dishonorable. Every child readily recognizes these two negative traits in Prince John from the popular childhood Robin Hood stories. While the character of Robin Hood is largely fictional, Prince John was a very real person who played a key role in history. John was the fourth son of Henry II, making him unlikely to ever rule. But through a series of events, the crown fell to Richard, with John being next in line. While both men had their issues, John's rapaciousness firmly fixed his reputation.

Both the Disney animated film and the classic Errol Flynn movie amplify this greed for money, the lust for power, and the effect it had on the community. John failed to understand that when you give, more will be given to you and conversely, when you take, even what you already have will be taken away. Richard did indeed banish his brother. And even when John eventually became king, his continued greed and lust for power cost him dearly, resulting in the Magna Carta, which permanently wrested full authority away from the king.

This proved true the musings of the fifth-century philosopher Boethius: "Wealth shines in giving rather than in hoarding: for the miser is hateful, whereas the generous man is applauded." French historian Léon Gautier attri-

---

1. Dhuoda, *Handbook for William: A Carolingian Woman's Counsel for Her Son*, trans. Carol Neel (Washington, D.C.: The Catholic University of America Press, 1999), p. 56, 62.

butes greed to the downfall of chivalry. "Love of riches had not only attacked the chivalrous orders, but in a very short space of time all knights caught the infection."[2]

Our boys need to understand that they never truly win when they are selfish. Greed blinds us to the needs of others and ends up coming back to bite us in the long run. Pursuing the way of generosity not only benefits others but helps the giver as well.

✝ Aim for Big-Heartedness

The virtue—the true chivalrous virtue—is liberality,
and to use the proper word, largesse.[3]　　—*Léon Gautier*

Gautier considered generosity one of the highest of chivalric virtues. He used the term *largesse*, a word that emerged into our lexicon in the thirteenth century. Largesse implies extravagant giving and a gallant spirit of altruism, charity, and living open-handed. In a nutshell, it is big-heartedness.

If nothing else, my boys want to be big. They want big muscles, big cars (eye roll), big everything. Their bear hugs mow me over, and when they are sold on an idea, nothing can stop them. Our aim as parents ought to be to encourage and cultivate big-heartedness.

Generosity is giving out of what you have, it implies a willing sacrifice made for others. As we seek to encourage

2. Léon Gautier, *Chivalry* (London: George Routledge and Sons, 1891), p. 78.
3. Gautier, *Chivalry*, p. 70.

our boys to be generous, we need to get to the core issues. Generosity is far more than making a donation to help someone or some cause, especially for a child. It is easy for us to give a little here and there and even easier for our children to be generous with Mommy and Daddy's money because there is not a cost to themselves. Our goal should be to help our boys see the bigger picture.

Big-hearted generosity includes a desire to give to others of one's time, self, possessions, etc. Challenging our boys to live out this lifestyle is simpler than you might think when we keep the bigger picture in mind. The chivalry challenge is the perfect place to work on this virtue.

A knight in training learns the value of being generous and sharing. We help him understand that this is not limited merely to being generous with his physical possessions but also being generous with his time and his affections. Ultimately, like so many other aspects of the knight's Code of Chivalry, it boils down to having an eye toward sharing with others. Generosity is not something imposed by others but rather should be birthed out of the heart. Knights-to-be need to be challenged to look for ways they can freely choose to be generous with those around them, whether it is sharing a toy with a sibling or giving that weary soul at the grocery store a contagious smile.

✢ The Science of Generosity

Many times we feel the benefits of generosity, but science is starting to unlock what is happening biologically when people form the habit of giving. We are finding that it causes hormonal reactions that make us happier and healthier, creating a cyclical effect that leads us to give again.

Dr. Christian Smith, who has dedicated his life to researching and analyzing the science behind giving writes,

> Generosity is paradoxical. Those who give, receive back in turn. By spending ourselves for others' well-being, we enhance our own standing. In letting go of some of what we own, we ourselves move toward flourishing. This is not only a philosophical or religious teaching; it is a sociological fact.... [In] failing to care for others, we do not properly take care of ourselves.[4]

When generosity becomes a way of life, overall health and longevity improve.

Conversely, we pay a steep price for not being generous. A 2010 study reveals that stingy behavior actually increases cortisol levels, meaning that people who are stingy experience higher levels of stress.[5] Being generous is not only the

---

4. Christian Smith, *The Paradox of Giving* (New York: Oxford University Press, 2014), p. 1.
5. Elizabeth Dunn, "On the Costs of Self-interested Economic Behavior How Does Stinginess Get under the Skin?," *Journal of Health Psychology* 15, no. 4 (2010): 627–33. Abstract available at hpq.sagepub.com/content/15/4/627.abstract.

right thing to do but helps everyone involved, both the recipient and the giver.

✦ Practice What You Preach

With children, generosity starts with learning how to share. Anyone who has been a parent for more than two minutes knows that this does not come naturally. For many young children, the words *no* and *mine* are two of the first words they learn. Helping our young pages learn how to share is exhausting. It takes time and training to help them recognize the benefits of big-heartedness and develop a habit of generosity.

How we go about doing it makes a huge difference. We must lead by example. Our children need to see us living open-handedly with others by being generous in sharing our time, our attention, and our finances. They need to see us sharing the abundance of what we have with others, even if we do not get anything in return.

This includes living generously with our own children. I do not mean giving our children whatever they want but rather giving them what they need. They need love and boundaries. They need patience and training. They actually do not need a whole lot of stuff, but they do need us. They must know that we are there for them and that we enjoy being with them.

In this day and age, our boys need to not hear us complain about them even though everyone else is doing it. It is easy to slip into whining and complaining about the inconveniences of life. It is easy to forget that the inconveniences we are complaining about are little people with souls. If we claim to want to care for the needy "out there" but only whine about caring for the needy in our own home, we walk the path of the hypocrite.

When someone tells you she cannot stand to be with her kids, you can choose to respond with a positive comment about children. When everyone else is sharing celebratory posts about the freedom a new school year provides by getting their kids out of the house, you can focus instead on the excitement of a fresh start and the opportunity your children have to learn new things. There is nothing wrong with wanting a break. You can even celebrate the opportunity to refuel so that you are ready to welcome your children home again. But the words we use to express that feeling impact those around us, especially our children.

Parenting takes an investment of time. It is hardly convenient. We get to invest generously into our boys' lives, cultivating their hearts, minds, and very souls. The perk of parenthood is that this endless giving will pay off down the road. As our children grow, that parent–child relationship will blossom into friendship. One day we will be old, and they will have an opportunity to live selflessly and care for us.

Think of it this way. We would count a person who devotes his life to helping the poor and needy as a generous person. We admire the sacrifice he is making. But if that person took to social media with constant complaints about the drudgery of his work and posted jubilant selfies every time he took a break from this generous work, what would we think of him? We certainly would not consider him generous or kind or noble.

The same holds true with our children. We are raising the next generation. It is hard. There may be days we hide in the closet eating dark chocolate and offering up desperate prayers. But we must watch how we communicate. Our kids need to know that we love them and that it is an honor to invest into their lives.

As we model this big-hearted giving in our very own homes, it will be easier for our knights-to-be to receive our encouragement to live in the same way with others. Modeling a generous life begins by being faithful in the mundane and ordinary moments of our lives.

✦ Developing the Habit: Training Is Essential

Modeling is not enough. Selfishness is deeply rooted and it takes both intentional training and a whole lot of practice before generosity can become a habit. We need to prepare our squires in advance for the scenarios they might face where they have the opportunity to live in a big-hearted way and then encourage them to embrace the in-the-moment opportunities they have to practice the art of generosity.

We must keep in mind our goal here. True generosity comes from the heart. It cannot be forced, but it must be trained. For instance, my sister made her children pool some of their own money together to buy a birthday gift for their younger brother. They did not jump for joy to give up their money, money that they had already earmarked for tasty treats or toys of their own. She held firm, however, and talked about the importance of giving and how excited their little brother would feel when he opened his gift. She told them how much more they would enjoy giving him this gift because there was an actual cost to them personally. They caught the vision and, in fact, became so engrossed in picking out the perfect gift that they ended up begging to spend even more of their own money.

There is a cost to big-hearted living. Had my sister not imposed this lesson, her kids would have missed out on the benefits they received from opening up their hands and hearts to give to someone else.

Spontaneous giving is birthed out of discipline, simply doing it because it is the right thing to do. Giving, as an act of the will, forms habits that start one down the path of a lifetime of generosity. Keeping the goal of heartfelt giving in mind helps us watch our tone. Instead of adopting a demanding tone, we are reminded that the purpose is training with their interests at heart.

✢ Sharing Is Caring

For our littlest ones, we make generous living concrete and relatable by teaching them to share their toys. This requires us to get down on the ground with them and walk through what it means to be courteous to others. Extending empathy during this process enables our sons to understand that we love them and want what is best for them as we teach them the give and take that marks a generous society.

When they are the recipients of generosity, we help them tune into their feelings and connect that to how others feel when they share those blocks or car with a friend.

It is interesting to find the balance here. We recognize that our kids have personal possessions. In our home we do not require sharing at all time and in every circumstance. We teach siblings to respect personal property boundaries for extra-special items. When friends come over, we might put that toy out of sight.

✦ Habit of Hospitality

Speaking of friends, cultivating the habit of hospitality early is a special gift we give to our children. We live in an era in which families are increasingly becoming islands, separated from extended family and even from the community. In the spirit of generosity, we seek to cultivate the vintage art of hospitality, by opening our homes and our hearts to those around us.

At its core, generosity is giving of ourselves.

When we invite people over, it gives our family the opportunity to put our guest's desires above our own. As adults, we get creative in conversation as we seek to find areas in common with new friends.

We help our children adopt big-hearted living by drawing them into the preparation process and showing where they can play an important role. They help tidy up the home and pull some snack or meal items together. As your children get older, allow for their personalities to shine. If you have one who is an artist, encourage him to make a welcome sign. If you have a social/leader type, charge him with pulling together a game plan for the event and think about activities that your guests might like to do.

Someone who excels at big-hearted living will take the needs of all into account, especially those who are younger. I would gather my boys around and tell them about who was going to come over, sharing names and ages. We would discuss what they might like to do when they arrived. We would baby-proof the house and collect toys we thought might be of particular interest. My boys would get excited about being the big kids and entertaining the little ones.

We give our boys a great gift, which they can then give to others, when we teach them how to converse with people of different ages. The same care should be taken in talking to your child about an adult who is visiting, by brainstorming in advance interesting questions your child might ask.

✤ Giving the Gift of a Smile

Have you ever stopped to people watch? It is amazing how many people race through life with a stressed look on their face and sometimes just outright frowns. We have no idea what someone else is going through, but we can teach our kids that one of the easiest gifts we can give is the gift of a smile. And that smile can virtually turn someone's day around.

I still remember the very first day I challenged my boys to give the gift of a smile. It was their mission for the day. For one of my boys a ready smile and a quick hello comes easily. This is the child who would flirt endlessly with anyone who would look his way when he was a baby and toddler. Another son was born scowling. I used to joke that those first two boys of mine made a great team. One would provide friendliness and manners while the other would make sure they did not get kidnapped.

As we set out to run errands that morning (specifically to find stuff to try to remove the crayon stains from all of our clothes due to a crayon that went through the dryer), we decided to take advantage of the opportunity to spread some smiles.

Mr. Grumpy Pants told me stubbornly in the parking lot that he did not have any smiles to give. Little did he realize that I could outsmart him! I pulled out the old competitive spirit and challenged the boys to see how many people they could say hello to in the store. Mr. Friendly jumped on board immediately and was smiling away. It did not take long for the other two boys to get into it as they came running up to whisper their smile count. It reminded me of that battle scene at Helm's Deep in one of *The Lord of the Rings* movies where Legolas the elf and Gimli the dwarf had a friendly rivalry going with their kill count. My boys did not need to see the movie for inspiration. The competitive spirit is simply hardwired into them.

"I smiled at that lady, Mommy," my youngest told me, beaming.

"Well, I smiled and said hi to that mother and her little boy," another added.

And so it continued until they all ran up to greet our check-out lady.

They received many smiles in return, and it was a good first day of learning the benefits of gifting a smile. That day set them down the path of big-heartedness in this area.

✝ The Gift in the Giving

We give gifts that are intangible such as a smile or some conversation or sometimes give a temporary gift, such as when we share a toy. But bringing our children into the gift of gift giving is also a great delight. Some families love to write notes, buy small trinkets, or make little gifts for each other. Our children see this and imitate.

When it comes to gift giving, it is important to emphasize the heart behind the gift, not the monetary value. Encouraging homemade gifts is a great way to accomplish this because it requires an investment of time, thought, and creativity.

While giving starts at home and among friends, we also want to connect our children to the great needs outside our immediate community. Blogger Amanda White set out to do just that with her children. She wanted her kids at a young age to experience giving to others that involved more than just sharing a cookie with a friend. She wanted to give them a heart to give to people around the world.

She wanted her kids to know that the comfortable life they enjoy in America is not the norm for most kids in other countries. She looked for concrete ways for her children to give. It started when her oldest was four and they read about the need for shoes in Haiti. They passed out a notice and bags for a shoe drive and ended up collecting over seven hundred pairs of shoes that they then shipped to Haiti. This prompted them to look for more ways to creatively get involved with giving to others.

Katherine and Isabelle Adams had a goal to raise $500 to partially fund a well in Ethiopia by selling hand-crafted origami ornaments at Starbucks in exchange for donations. Within two months, they had raised over $10,000, starting a whole movement.

Our neighbors recently invited us to their lemonade stand where the kids were raising money for a local children's hospital. Other friends put together bags full of essentials to hand out to the homeless in their area. The key is to make it concrete and something that specifically involves our children in the process of giving.

When giving becomes a habit, it becomes a natural way of life. A while back I was having one of those rough days. You know, the kind of day when you just wake up on the wrong side of the bed and want to run away from the world. After getting snarly and impatient with the boys, I retreated to my bedroom discouraged. I needed some time alone with God. Soon I heard a soft knock. Wiping the tears away, I invited my sons into my room. Three boys walked in with bashful smiles while my little girl twirled around them giggling. They handed me a homemade bracelet with a note and three pieces of chocolate attached. They had each donated a mini candy bar from their candy stash and written a note that read, "We love you and are glad you're our mom." In addition to the homemade gift, they gave me forgiveness.

✞ Throwing Down the Gauntlet

Faithfully giving in small ways during childhood paves the way for a continued living with largesse as they become adults. We want to raise big-hearted boys: boys marked by open hands and generous living. So let's put this into practice. Here are some ideas to get you started. Be sure to jot down ideas of your own and really personalize this aspect of the code to fit your family and community.

- ✦ Talk to your boys about what it means to be generous. What is largesse? Encourage your kids to brainstorm some ways they could live out big-heartedness.
- ✦ Point out when others act in big-hearted ways.
- ✦ Have your son pick a sibling or friend and surprise him by doing one of his chores.
- ✦ Challenge them to give the gift of a smile when you are at the store.

✦ Suggest that your boys let the person behind them in line go first: at the drinking fountain, at the store, at the park, and so on.

✦ Encourage your knights in training to rake a neighbor's leaves, shovel snow from her walk, or sweep her driveway.

✦ Help your sons prepare a meal for someone who is sick, a family with a new baby, or someone who just moved.

✦ Make a habit of meeting new neighbors and bringing them cookies.

✦ Have your boys offer to return shoppers' carts at the grocery store parking lot.

Sharing

✦ Review with your kids why we share with others.

✦ Help your boys choose a toy to share with a friend or sibling.

Hospitality

✦ Plan a party. Teach your sons how to be a generous host. Your knights-to-be will also have an opportunity to:

   ▪ Learn how to greet guests.

   ▪ Share toys (put away an extra-special one, but be generous with the rest).

■ Plan with guests in mind. Talk about their likes or dislikes and plan out things to do that your guests will enjoy (games, activities, toys to highlight).

✦ Learn how to talk to a grandparent or a great-grandparent. Spend some time together, giving the gift of conversation.

Gifts

✦ **Homemade gifts.** Jot down ideas for homemade gifts. Grandparents and aunts and uncles love original artwork. Brainstorm ways to make these creations gift worthy. Here are a few ideas to get the creative juices flowing:

■ Homemade cards
■ Fingerprint stationery
■ Photo gifts (always a hit with grandparents)
■ Hand-picked flowers

✦ If you give your child an allowance, establish the habit of giving early. Set up a gift fund—to buy gifts for friends and family as well as a tithe or charity fund. Our children designate 10 percent as a tithe for church or a ministry and 10 percent toward a Christmas and birthday gift fund.

Outreach and Charity

✦ Participate with Operation Christmas Child to collect a shoebox full of gifts to be sent overseas to a child in another country.

✦ Volunteer at a food bank or outreach facility.

✦ Come up with creative ways your child could fundraise for the ministry of his choice, such as

 ▪ Doing extra chores.

 ▪ Making things to sell.

 ▪ Loose change drive (conducted by your sons).

CHAPTER 14

The Code: Persevere

> ✚ *Persevere and Finish the Task at Hand*
>
> A knight sets about with determination to finish the task at hand. He reminds himself to stick with his task before embarking on play or another assignment.

"BE ON YOUR GUARD," fair Una warned George as they entered her kingdom. Body tensed and eyes alert, he made his way toward the tall brass tower the people had built to protect themselves against raids from the fierce dragon.

With the enthusiasm of youth and the resolve of character, George eagerly embraced this new quest. Having never fought a dragon before, he had no idea what lay ahead. But he was ready. According to the Saint George and the Dragon story, he did not have long to wait, for at the sight of his approach, the dragon reared up "high, monstrous, horrible, and vast." In breathtaking detail, we are swept into the heart of this battle. Like most battles, there was no quick victory as they clashed—both fierce, strong, and determined.

My boys listen, breathless with anticipation, every time we read this tale. Every. Single. Time. George was thrown down, battered, and worn. Yet he arose after each setback to continue the fight. Finally, one of his blows pierced the dragon's wing as the beast seethed and "like a wide devouring oven, sent a flame of fire that scorched the knight's face and heated his armor red-hot" before retreating for the day. Weary and wounded the knight fell.

But this battle was not over. The next morning he arose, refreshed and ready to engage once more in the battle that lasted for two more days before the persistent knight succeeded in vanquishing his foe.

This story was meant to inspire the knights of old to persevere—to stick to their mission. It continues to inspire us today.

✦ Why Perseverance Matters

The knights of old possessed grit. They used their strength and discipline not only to begin brave quests but also to see them through to completion. They persevered at whatever it took to finish a task, even when it was challenging, even when it seemed hopeless; thus they garnered a reputation of dependability. Honor always and victory often followed those who did not give up.

Developing this discipline should be a critical component of a squire's training. Faithfulness in small aspects during childhood will foster the control and determination to complete larger and more important tasks as he gets older. Perseverance is needed now more than ever in this distracted day and age when we are pulled in multiple directions by competing activities, opportunities, and devices.

Ralph Waldo Emerson said, "A hero is no braver than an ordinary man, but he is braver five minutes longer." Perseverance sets an extraordinary man apart from an ordinary one, and it is this vision that we want to pass on to our boys.

Perseverance is steadfastness in a course of action despite difficulty, setbacks, or delays in achieving success. It is an attitude, a mind-set that does not quit but is determined, disciplined, and creative in working toward solutions. While passion is important to get going, persistence is what keeps us chasing our passions even in the face of difficulties. Because we live in an insta-everything culture we need to be more mindful than ever to encourage our children to persevere.

The secret to success in life is not primarily talent, but rather a blend of passion and persistence, something psychologist and researcher Dr. Angela Duckworth calls *grit*. As she explains in her book *Grit: The Power and Passion of Perseverance*, "grit is having stamina. Grit is sticking with your future, day-in, day-out." Raising kids who persevere is about so much more than academics or future vocation. It is about the process of becoming the people they are meant to be. It is preparing them for all of life.

The opportunities to power this message home are everywhere. Just the other day, my husband gave one of our boys *the* look. You know, that mischievous look that communicates, "You had better run because I'm going to get you." Our son was off like a shot, grabbing hold of the banister to make the turn quicker as he bounded up the steps, my hubby high-tailing it after him. Moments later I heard a high-pitched prepubescent squeal as my hubby threw out sage advice between tickles. "Never, ever stop on the stairs. You lost your momentum."

It is important for our kids to know that success does not always go to the strongest or the smartest, but to the one who sticks to a task until they figure it out. They need to see how this plays out for others, which is why reading is so important. Our kids are inspired when they read biographies of people like Thomas Edison who never gave up and who declared, "I have not failed, but rather found 10,000 ways it won't work." He persevered and gave us the gift of the lightbulb. They find courage to keep going when they read of Abraham Lincoln's unflagging desire to learn and try new things or his many failed attempts at running for political office before finding eventual victories.

When we connect hard work with success and satisfaction we set them on the road to embody that mind-set too. Faithfulness and tenacity, the two elements that described knights of valor, ought to be what we all aspire to today. Encouraging our boys to embark on exciting quests as they learn new skills and work toward independence builds eagerness for the process of learning. We dust them off when they fall, give them a hand up when necessary, and become the voice in their head that inspires them to keep going.

✟ Weathering the Storms of Life

When my close friend Amanda Ippel recalls her childhood, she remembers a string of defeats and failures. She tried out for cheerleading and did not make the team. She tried color guard, theater, volleyball, and other activities, looking to find her niche. The actual failures and letdowns are not what dominate her memories, however, but rather the way her parents modeled how to react to them.

"Keep trying, trying, trying," they would tell her. "Anything worth having is worth working for." When another disappointment would surface they were there to encourage her and remind her to not let those setbacks phase her. They reiterated that life does not come to you on a silver platter. You have to work for it.

In eleventh grade, Ippel came home, announcing with triumph that she had finally landed a part in the school musical. She and her mom both cried. Her persistence had paid off.

Her parents acknowledged that life is full of adversity, but declared that how they respond was entirely up to them. Ippel is certain that if she had been coddled as a child, told she was a victim of bullying, unfair teachers, or coaches who played favorites, she would have floundered when the real storms of life would hit one day.

While we all encounter obstacles that demand perseverance to navigate through, some are fiercer than others. Ippel's big storm hit on May 20, 2012. One minute she was
laughing with her husband and the next minute searing pain
hit and her face went slack. She remembers her husband immediately calling 911 and telling them that he thought his
wife was having a stroke. *This is silly,* she thought. *Who has a
stroke at twenty-nine?* Miraculously, she survived. But her
life and the lives of her family would be forever altered.
This capable and energetic mother of four with one more
on the way had to fight for everything. As she sat in the
hospital, propped up by pillows and unable to move on her
own, she realized she could sit there and feel sorry for herself or she could get up (figuratively speaking) and move forward. She credits her faith, her family, and that tenacious
spirit her parents cultivated within her for her success.

Perseverance became a way of life, not only for her, but
for her family as well. They all answered the call in extraordinary ways. Step by step, Ippel learned how to sit up, how
to walk, how to eat, and even how to open a door.

Looking back, she sees how God used her experience in
more ways than she could have imagined. Her children had
a front-row seat to persevering in the midst of adversity. It
was especially hard on her oldest son. She spoke words of
truth and hope, "This isn't the life we wanted or planned
for, son. But we can and will move forward." Although doc-
tors predicted that she would never be able to care for her
children again, she fights each day to regain her independence. She is proving them wrong.

✦ Preparing to Persevere

Parents and other authority figures in a child's life play a key role in developing the foundation of perseverance. Time and again, research has illustrated that parents who are warm and nurturing as well as firm raise kids who thrive.[1] We are called to be benevolent rulers, providing clear boundaries and leadership within the context of a caring relationship.

Finding balance is the key. A parent who veers toward the extremes of permissive parenting can hamper the development just as much as a parent who leans toward the other extreme of being too authoritarian. Understanding your propensity to lean in one direction or the other will guide you back to finding balance in parenting. It also helps us understand why there can be such a spectrum of parenting styles. Every parent and every child is unique. You need to home in on your individual children's needs as well as your strengths and weaknesses as a parent to help them become resilient warriors.

When it comes to perseverance, our children thrive when they are loved unconditionally and pushed to persevere, to not give up in the face of challenges.

"I can't do it" my son screamed, pounding his fists down

---

1. Wendy S. Grolnick and Richard M. Ryan, "Parent Styles Associated with Children's Self-Regulation and Competence in School," *Journal of Educational Psychology* 81 (1989): 143–54. Laurence Steinberg, "Presidential Address: We Know Some Things: Parent-Adolescent Relationships in Retrospect and Prospect," *Journal of Research on Adolescence* 11 (2011): 1–19.

on the keyboard. After working on a new song for an up-coming recital, he was frustrated with his progress. "I quit."

He stiffened as I put my arm around his shoulder and urged him over to the couch. I let him emote a bit more before asking him why he was taking piano lessons in the first place.

"To learn how to play," he muttered. I felt as if I were in a scene from *Batman Begins*: After falling into an old well and breaking his arm, Bruce Wayne is carried back to the house. His father asks Bruce why we fall and then explains, "so we can learn to pick ourselves up."

Life is full of setbacks, and people, especially our little people, often just need a reminder to stand back up and keep going. Whether our kids react with anger, weeping, or listlessness, the temptation to give up is strong. As parents, it is our job to help them navigate through life. We encourage them lovingly and tenaciously until ours is the voice they hear in their head when they fall.

"I think I can, I think I can," is the refrain echoing in my head. Every single time we wanted to give up, my mom would refer back to that line in the book *The Little Engine That Could*. Helping our kids succeed does not mean we do things for them, but rather that we come alongside them and cheer them on. We encourage them to press ahead, knowing we believe in them.

✳ The Pitfalls of Praise

Thomas Edison wrote much about the importance of perseverance. Throughout his life, Edison operated under four principles taught to him by his mother.

1. Never get discouraged if you fail. Learn from it. Keep trying.
2. Learn with both your head and hands.
3. Not everything of value in life comes from books; experience the world.
4. Never stop learning. Read the entire panorama of literature.

Edison's mother instilled in her son what Stanford psychologist Dr. Carol Dweck refers to as a "growth mind-set." We need to encourage our boys, to be that voice in their head, but we must be mindful what that voice is saying. Teaching our sons to embrace challenges is of utmost importance. Instead of praising a child for his intelligence or talent, we ought to praise effort and creative problem solving. We need to help our kids view setbacks, not as failures, but as opportunities to learn.

Dweck warns parents about the pitfalls of praise. "Parents think they can hand children permanent confidence—like a gift—by praising their brains and talent. It doesn't work, and in fact has the opposite effect."[2] We must praise the process rather than the person.

2. Carol Dweck, *Mindset* (New York: Ballantine, 2007), p. xx.

She and her colleagues conducted a study that demonstrated this effect. They gave over four hundred fifth graders from around the country an easy test made up of ten questions, puzzles, and riddles. Afterward, half of the kids were praised for their intelligence. "Wow! You must be really smart." The other half were praised for their effort. "Wow! You must have worked really hard on that quiz."

Next came a new test. But this time the students had a choice. They could select a harder version, which they were told would provide a great opportunity to learn and grow, or another test similar to the first one. Only 33 percent of the students who were praised for their intelligence chose the more difficult test. But 92 percent of the second group who had been praised for their effort chose the harder option.

Then they gave the students a third test, one that was impossible to solve. The researchers wanted to see how the different kids attacked this challenge. The "effort" group worked hard and long before finally giving up and enjoyed themselves in the process. The "smart" group became easily frustrated and quickly gave up.

Finally, they concluded the study by bringing the students back and giving them a quiz similar to the first one. What they discovered blew them away. The "smart" group saw a 20 percent drop in their scores compared to the first test they took. The "effort" group saw a nearly 30 percent increase in scores, leading to a nearly 50 percent performance gap simply because of how the children were praised.[3]

---

3. C. M. Mueller and C. S. Dweck, "Intelligence Praise Can Undermine Motivation and Performance," *Journal of Personality and Social Psychology* 75 (1998): 33–52.

Our words matter. A person praised for his intelligence wants to preserve that reputation. He tends to play it safe and thus limits his potential. On the other hand, a person praised for his effort is inspired to seek new challenges.

✢ Foundations in Perseverance

So what can we do to encourage a persevering mind-set? We lay down the foundations when we honor our squire's desire to "do it myself." A wise parent never does for a child what the child can accomplish on his own. We affirm this desire by encouraging our kids to take on new challenges. This might mean that you restrain yourself from intervening, even if it takes your child three times longer to do something. When he makes mistakes, and he will, we encourage his progress and value the process over the finished product.

We build a habit of perseverance by helping him develop good habits. We are all creatures of habit; it is simply a matter of whether we have good habits or bad ones. Good habits will, as Charlotte Mason puts it, act as rails on which a person's life can run smoothly.

Developing the habit of self-regulation is key. Self-regulation is a person's ability to control his behavior and impulses, follow directions, and persist on a task. It is the ability to pay attention and to focus.

An increasing amount of research on self-regulation has highlighted the importance of this critical skill. According to Dr. Megan McClelland, children who enter formal schooling without the ability to pay attention, remember instructions, and demonstrate self-control have more difficulty throughout the rest of their academic pursuits and into their careers.[4] Studies show that lack of self-regulation skills hinders their ability to finish what they start and make healthy choices in life.[5]

Although some personalities might have an easier time adopting self-regulatory habits, it is possible for everyone to develop self-control and the ability to delay gratification, even our active and impulsive little boys. Just as a boy will want to develop his physical muscles, he can build the muscles of self-control. The more he flexes and works those muscles, the stronger they will become.

✦ Equipping Our Kids to Succeed

Challenging our young knights in training to persevere includes equipping them to succeed. In a world where boys seem to be floundering—lazy and lacking purpose—we need to take a different approach. Whereas girls are more

4. M. M. McClelland, C. E. Cameron, S. B. Wanless, and A. Murray, "Executive Function, Self-regulation, and Social-emotional Competence: Links to School Readiness." In O. N. Saracho and B. Spodek, eds., *Contemporary Perspectives on Research in Social Learning Self-regulation and Academic Achievement in the Transition to School* (Charlotte, NC: Information Age Publishing, 2007).

5. M. M. McClelland, A. Acock, A. Piccinin, S. A. Rhea, and M. C. Stallings, "Relations between Preschool Attention Span-Persistence and Age 25," *Early Childhood Research Quarterly* 28, no. 2 (2013): 314–24. Walter Mischel, T. R. Schlam, N. L. Wilson, Y. Shoda, O. J. Ayduk, "Preschoolers' Delay of Gratification Predicts Their Body Mass 30 Years Later," *Journal of Pediatrics* 162 (2013): 90–93.

likely to do things to please people, boys want to do something real and big. They want to see results. They want to know why. We can motivate our boys to persevere and to apply themselves, we simply have to market it differently.

Passion is a powerful motivator. Passion is fueled by purpose and fueled through perseverance. Connecting our boys to a grander purpose for their life infuses meaning. That in turn develops passion and spurs persistence toward their goals. Our boys thrive when they have a sense of purpose, when they know that what they are doing matters. That helps them stick to even mundane tasks and overcome setbacks.

✛ Building the Habits of Attention: Play and Work

Creating time in your child's schedule for self-directed play has many surprising benefits. Play is the work of childhood. It is this spontaneous and imaginative realm in which children first work out lessons in perseverance as they work toward creative innovations and experience the pleasure of pushing through. Learning perseverance is a natural by-product of self-directed play. They do not need lessons on this from us, but rather the freedom to pursue their play.

When there is pleasure in the process, it is easy for the brain to flex those focus muscles. A child becomes engrossed in building a tower of blocks. When it falls over, he might express frustration, but left to his own without other activities to distract him, he has the opportunity to tackle it again and again, and find a better way to build.

Let a playing child play. When he is engrossed in the work of play, refrain from interrupting so he can retain and strengthen his natural focus. Turning off distractions such as an overscheduled life and reliance on screens for entertainment will cultivate these opportunities for organic perseverance exercises.

We do not, however, just leave a child to indulge only his own whims. We cultivate self-discipline and the habits of attention by giving him real work around the home. Boys want to know that their contribution makes a difference. Hal and Melanie Young, authors of *Raising Real Men*, advocate issuing the challenge by giving boys the hardest jobs that they are physically capable of doing. Challenge them rather than give them easy or inconsequential jobs. Encourage them to rise to the occasion and then thank them for the impact they are having.

Matthew Jacobson, father to four boys, believes that modeling and encouraging the development of a strong work ethic is important. He too gives his sons hard work to do and frequently reminds them, "Men work until the job is done." He gently points them back to their chores when they get distracted and affirms the effort they put into their work. Afterward comes the satisfaction of seeing the fruit of one's labor.

✝ Building the Habits of Attention: The Power of Focus

Perseverance is impeded without a developed ability to focus. Stick-to-itiveness requires an intense level of concentration.

Boys are action oriented. They *need* to *move*. We all know this because we live with it every day. This constant need to move actually serves a purpose because movement wires the brain to learn. It helps develop strong connections between the two hemispheres of the brain, making learning easier. It activates the cerebellum, which makes learning faster, and it provides an important boost of oxygen to the brain enabling boys to think and engage in complex problem solving.[6]

As parents and teachers, it is important to recognize the need for and value of movement. It is even more important that we help our boys start to recognize this too. This has been a game changer in our home and in the homes of hundreds of families I have counseled over the years.

Using movement is just one of the weapons we have in our arsenal to improve focus and move forward toward this objective. Putting this struggle into battle terms helps boys understand what is at stake and to use movement to fight for focus. When our boys are distracted, getting up and moving can be just what they need to wake up their brains.

---

6. Heather Haupt, *The Ultimate Guide to Brain Breaks* (Gilbert: Cultivated Lives, 2013).

Taking a few minutes for a brain break helps clear the mental cobwebs. The first time I did this with one of my boys, I mimicked an army sergeant and barked out orders to "drop and give me twenty." He laughed, but did it and then bounced back into his assignment with renewed vigor.

When our young pages are struggling to work on a complex math problem or writing assignment, it helps if they take a walk and talk it out. Methodical movement during the thinking process does wonders to unlock the mind's ability to find innovative solutions.

I remind my boys that these are tools they can use whenever necessary to push through and persevere at whatever they are doing. Our goal as parents is to help our children naturally do what is needed for them to retain focus and mental clarity. Once they master this, it will pay huge dividends in just about every area of life.

As they get older, introduce the power of a to-do list and teach your boys to effectively break a big project down into manageable, bite-size pieces. Remind them to not worry about the entire seemingly insurmountable project, but instead focus on the next thing. Teaching them how to step back and see the big picture before breaking it down into smaller goals enables them to muster the courage and fortitude to see a project through to completion.

T. S. Eliot reminds us of the importance of risk and the value of failure: "Only those who will risk going too far can possibly find out how far one can go." It is so easy to want to bail out our knights in training and rescue them from the momentary discomfort of failures or mistakes. But we must let them make this walk. Here is the thing that they need to know about failure; here's truth we need to revisit over and over again as our boys move out bravely into new territory and unknown adventures: *Failure is the best way to learn.* If you do not try and fail, you do not learn. If you do not learn, you will never change.

We need to remind our children that failure is not final. It is only final if you remain where you have fallen. Attempting something new will seem impossible until it is done. The adventure lies in the attempt and the triumph in the overcoming.

✤ Throwing Down the Gauntlet

Communication

Read Stories of Resilience

- ✦ Biographies almost always feature examples of perseverance because it is the hallmark of all success.
- ✦ More book recommendations are in the resource section at the end of the book.

Try Dinnertime Conversation Starters That Highlight Perseverance

- ✦ What did you learn today?
- ✦ What problems did you encounter and how did you work through them?

✦ What mistake did you make today that taught you something?

Develop a Growth Mind-Set Vocabulary

✦ Instead of saying, "I'm not good at this," say "What am I missing?"
✦ Instead of saying, "I give up," say "I'll use some of the strategies we've learned."
✦ Instead of saying, "I failed," say "I haven't figured this out *yet!*"
✦ Instead of saying "This is too hard," say "This may take some time and effort."

Persevering Is Doing Something That Takes a While

✦ Think of a skill that your child will really have to work at and encourage him to stick with it, even when it gets hard (such as cooking, washing the car, doing yard work).
✦ Music lessons teach our boys that daily practice takes them from novices to masters.

Teach Them How to Be Brave and Tackle a New Challenge; Give Them a Voice to Hear in Their Head

✦ Read *The Little Engine that Could*. Encourage your sons by having them say, "I think I can, I think I can." When they have persevered, have them say, "I knew I could."

✦ Have your squires memorize this saying: If at first I don't succeed, try, try again.

✦ Change how you talk about *results* by emphasizing effort over talent.

The Habit of Focus

Move When You Are Not Focused or Persevering

✦ Take a quick brain break: do some jumping jacks, push-ups, or run around the backyard.

✦ If you need to work out a big problem, talk it out on a walk.

✦ Stand up at the kitchen counter to work on a challenging problem.

Teach Them the Art of Making To-Do Lists

✦ For a child who is not reading yet, make a picture-based to-do list. (You could even laminate it and let him check off boxes with a dry erase marker.)

✦ Develop routines and help your boys to stick to them. (Try a morning routine and a bedtime routine to start with.)

✦ Help your son break down a big job into smaller parts and then work with him to stick to the routine until the job is done. (For example, cleaning his room could consist of putting books away first, then clothes, then shoes, then toys by type.)

Challenge Your Child to Learn a New Skill, Something That Will Take Practice to Learn

✦ How to tie or lace shoes.

✦ How to zip up a coat.

✦ How to button up a shirt

✦ How to wash a car well.

✦ How to make cookies or cook something else all by himself (multiple steps and the art of baking involved).

Develop Self-Regulation Skills

✦ **Extra chores.** Make a list of extra jobs he could do to earn money for something special.

✦ **Balance races.** Play games that require kids to persevere with focus, either a race while balancing a beanbag on his head or while balancing a plastic ball or egg on a spoon. If you are brave, make it a real egg!

✦ **Red light, green light.** A quintessential children's game; when someone calls green light, the kids can go (run, walk, jump, hop), and when red light is called the children must stop and freeze. Give it a medieval twist by calling out knight and knave. To maximize the development of self-regulation skills, mix it up by reversing the two so green means stop and red means go.

✝ CHAPTER 15

The Code:
Pursue Excellence

> ✝ *Pursue Excellence in All You Do*
>
> A valiant knight pursues excellence in every challenge he faces. He shows exceptional valor, bravery, and skill. He hones his strengths and becomes the best at what he does.

THE NEWS HIT HARD. William Marshal, the boy who had been all but abandoned by his father due to broken promises years earlier, had toiled and embraced his training with a focused ferocity to be the best knight possible. He achieved knighthood earlier than most and fought valiantly in those early campaigns. But peace reigned now and the need for ready warriors had decreased. His lord no longer needed his services.

He was a warrior without a cause to fight for, a knight

without a lord to serve. He had two choices: strive to make his way in the world and fight for a future or take the easy way of returning to his brother's estate and embrace the life of a "hearth son."

Loafing young men are not simply a twenty-first-century phenomenon. Most nobles passed their titles and the entirety of their lands to the oldest son, leaving younger sons with nothing. Noble sons without title could either pursue a career in the church or as a knight or simply live within their family's estate. Enough younger sons chose this easy route of living in luxury and comfort at home that the English law books refer to them as hearth sons. Without title or money of their own however, these men were not able to marry and support a family. They had no future.

What was going through William Marshal's mind as he faced this dilemma? He was next in line to inherit the family estate. Choosing the path of a hearth son would be a comfortable life, but one without honor and purpose unless something happened to his elder brother. With determination, he chose the harder path—continuing to pursue his calling and taking that attitude of excellence into everything he did. He possessed little, but compensated with grit and dignity. Soon he became known and respected in the tournaments where he gradually worked his way up from his impoverished state.

His commitment to excellence, or prowess, opened many doors for him. Nothing held him back. This tenacity coupled with his unflagging loyalty caught the attention of Eleanor of Aquitaine, wife of King Henry II. She appointed him to personally train the crown prince. Commitment to excellence never goes unnoticed and this man who had set out to prove he was more than just a forgotten younger son now trained the king's oldest son. From there he would come to serve a total of five kings and concluded his career as regent, in command of all England until King John's nine-year-old son came of age to rule. William's commitment to excellence was unflagging. In his old age, he made provisions for each of his ten children, including his five daughters and his younger sons.

✠ Prowess: The Pursuit of a True Knight

Geoffroi de Charny was passionate about the pursuit of prowess—the display of exceptional ability, strength, and skill, especially in battle. At that time knights were becoming lazy and focusing on living a comfortable life rather than the challenge of pursuing an excellent one. De Charny went so far as to suggest that those who were not wholeheartedly pursuing excellence in their work were unworthy of the title of knight.

The mark of a knight is not mediocrity, but excellence; chivalry encompasses this wholehearted pursuit. For the knight, this meant investing great effort and attention, not just in battle but in all the aspects of chivalry. This pursuit of excellence enabled him to perform many mighty acts and in the process allowed him to recognize his most powerful abilities. As a knight homed in on what he did best, he pursued that gift, whether it was fighting on horseback, wielding the sword, or guiding others into battle. Maximizing his effectiveness in this way, he set himself apart as especially skilled in a particular field.

From the moment a boy became a page, he cultivated an attitude of excellence in all of his pursuits. Over the years, this attitude aided his progression through his training as he perfected his knightly craft and discovered his specific talents. Likewise, our boys should bring this approach into their everyday lives. They are to give any endeavor their best effort; as they pursue excellence in all things they will discover their unique areas of ability. As we raise our boys, we must charge them to pursue knighthood rather than settle for the easy path of a hearth son. Becoming a knight means taking on the mind-set of excellence.

✠ Prowess Builds on Perseverance

Excellence comes with dedication, determination, and a whole lot of practice. But perseverance alone does not always lead to excellence. My piano instructor of eleven years and the man who started teaching my boys music would chide his students, "Practice does not make perfect. Perfect practice makes perfect." He was always hammering home the idea of practicing well. Perseverance is not enough. Our sons need to understand that simply plodding along is not always the answer. You need to be sure you are walking with purpose and going in the right direction. It requires us to engage our hearts, our minds, and our bodies. It is the melding of passion, intelligence, and physical action.

If you drill a song a hundred times, but do not play it correctly, the only thing you accomplish is mastering the wrong way to play. The same goes for sports, or anything else for that matter. If you create the habit of throwing a ball wrong through constant repetition, you are not working toward learning and improving, but rather solidifying habits that will be even harder to break later.

Helping our children understand how and when to slow down and focus on doing something right the first time is vital. We do this by celebrating the process of editing and refining a project until it is just right. To become really good at something, you need to work hard and work consistently. Persevering well produces excellence.

✛ Cultivating the Pursuit of Excellence

Excellence is an art won by training and habituation . . . we are what we repeatedly do. Excellence, then, is not an act, but a habit.   —*Will Durant,* The Story of Philosophy

There is no easy way to say this. Instilling habits of excellence starts and ends with parents; it requires blood, sweat, and tears as we toil in the trenches with our children. But it is worth the effort. Being nurturing while setting high expectations helps our children persevere and instills a habit of excellence.

Look around you and find people who live their lives and pursue their work with passion and excellence. Ask them what their parents did to instill these habits and get ready to take notes. You will find a pattern of parents who worked hard themselves and parents who required their kids to diligently give their best effort. You will find parents who did not give up on their children or settle for half-done work, but rather parents who expected their children to rise to the occasion.

What does this look like in the early years? Yes, we inspire them with stories of knights, athletes, inventors, and explorers and people who pursued excellence. But more important than that, we are relentless in providing opportunities for our children to pursue excellence in their daily lives. Thomas Edison told us that "opportunity is missed by most people because it is dressed in overalls and looks like work." We have the opportunity as parents to instill in our children habits of excellence, but this is going to take an investment of time and effort on our part.

✠ Foundations

The most important thing we can do in the early years to build a foundation of doing a job well is to give our boys real, physical work to do. From the moment my boys could toddle around, they were assigned dirty diaper duty. That's right. They had to carry their soiled diapers out to the trash can. Even though I walked alongside them, it was their job to dispose of that stinky mess. I never asked them if they wanted to, I simply told them they would, keeping my tone positive and resolute. I would admire how big they were getting now that they could do big boy work. Sometimes they would toss their load and miss the target. Close was not good enough; it needed to make it inside the trash can.

As we give our children chores to do around the house and require quality execution, they begin to learn the habit of excellence. We can praise their effort *and* point out the job well done. With the diapers, I would always thank them and point out how nice it was that the room did not stink anymore. We take this attitude into teaching them how to take out the trash, how to put away their toys, how to hang up their clothes, and how to clean a bathroom.

There are endless rounds of quality control. I will never forget the time my youngest boy complained about having nothing to wear. After investigating the situation, I found two weeks of clean laundry stuffed behind the door in his closet. Busted. His brothers went outside to play with friends while he put each item away correctly and spent the rest of the afternoon in his room.

Back in Chapter 7, we discussed the importance of inspecting our children's work. By what is inspected, they will know what is expected. You will need to decide what the standards are for your family, provide proper instruction, and then inspect your boys' work to make sure it passes muster. Follow-up is critical for cultivating this foundation of excellence. This takes more work up front than if you did it yourself, but you are preparing your knight in training for independence and giving him the opportunity to make valuable contributions to the family in the meantime.

✝ Going the Extra Mile

But we do not want work just to pass muster. We have an opportunity during our sons' childhood to talk about the importance of exceeding expectations. An ideal knight is one who always goes the extra mile. This attitude of excellence permeated the entire idea of chivalry—extravagant devotion, generous giving, and truthfulness despite personal cost. They were not just to protect the weak who begged their protection but to be on the lookout for the needs of others.

Training our children to pursue excellence in their work now, will pave the way for success later in life. Recently we were talking to one of the snack ladies at Costco. She joked about how the boys should step up by helping with the dishes. My boys quickly announced that they do *all* the dishes, in disbelief that all other kids do not. (Shhhh, don't tell them this isn't the norm.) This kind lady reacted in surprise and then told us about her oldest son. She trained him from an early age to help out around the house, giving special attention to helping properly clean a bathroom. During his first week working for a restaurant, he came home astonished at the state of the restrooms. "Mom, they don't know how to clean a bathroom. It was awful." She told us that she encouraged him to step in and show them how to do it well. His willingness to do the dirty jobs, and do it well, led to promotions at work and soon he was managing the place. Building a work ethic in the younger years paves the way for success.

✤ Do Your Best. Be Your Best.

Expectations have an amazing way of fulfilling themselves. Set the bar low, you will get low results. Set the bar high, and boys will rise to the challenge. They are capable of far more than we generally give them credit for.

When I was growing up, my parents set high standards. They encouraged us to aim high, to live full out, and to always do our best. The goal was not perfection but rather doing the very best that we could. In my home, I frequently turn to sports references. While watching the Olympics we pointed out that the runners raced full speed until they passed the finish line. They did not slow down during the final approach; in fact, they usually had a burst of effort at the end. Excellence involves giving your all until it is finished.

During a recent discussion, I asked my young squires to imagine that a coach was giving out directions to perform a drill—say kicking a soccer ball around some cones. The coach models how it is done. Player 1 does the drill exactly as instructed. Player 2 pushes himself to see if he can do the drill faster. Player 3 focuses on both speed and accuracy, and ends the drill by practicing a shot into the net. Which player would improve the most? Who would the coach call on when the team needs a last-minute victory? It clicked.

In our home, we remind each other, "Not someday, but every day, in every way, we do our best, we give our all." In challenging our kids to pursue excellence we find ourselves repeating this mantra on a weekly or even daily basis.

Young Audie Murphy longed to fight. World War II was in full swing and this young Texas farm boy yearned to protect his country. He was only seventeen. Laughed at and told he would not amount to anything, this plucky boy set about to prove everyone wrong. He returned from war three years later the most decorated hero of World War II. He even received the highest military award for bravery given to any individual in the United States. The Medal of Honor is awarded for acts of conspicuous gallantry at the risk of one's own life, in going above and beyond the call of duty. Time and again, when others held back and situations appeared dire, Murphy would rush in to rescue a fellow soldier or capture a critical post. He was truly a modern-day knight.

His movie *To Hell and Back* gave our family a front-row seat to the importance of an attitude of excellence and perseverance. Boys need help connecting these inspiring stories to everyday moments in their own lives. As parents, we want to look for opportunities to challenge our children to try new things, to push themselves, to play all-out. We need to connect their intense, focused effort with the sense of pride in a job well done, whether that is a project at school, chores at home, building friendships on the playground, or playing hard on the sports field. They can embody the spirit of Audie Murphy.

✢ Cultivating the Gift

To properly pursue excellence, we need to reject the jack-of-all-trades mentality that has come to typify modern living. Less is more. While young children do need to have a variety of experiences, frenetic activity is counterproductive. Slowing down our lives and our schedules allows us and our children to focus on doing a few things well, allowing them to explore something deeply.

How do we cultivate the gifts within each of our children and set them on the path of excellence? I asked my friend Louisa about her childhood because I admire her family so much. She is one of five children. Early in life her parents focused on developing habits of perseverance and excellence with household chores and in school. They set the standard high, knowing their children were capable of the challenge. Her parents did not put much stock into making sure they grew up to be well-rounded individuals. The children did not pursue all the extracurricular options out there, though they all took music lessons and some were involved with sports. Instead of doing everything, her parents spent time really getting to know each of their children individually, discovering their interests and desires, and noticing their natural talents. As their children went into the teen years, they looked for opportunities to cultivate those gifts and hone skills in areas of interest. Each teen volunteered for a year before he or she found a paying job. This allowed them to pursue internship opportunities in vocational areas of interest. Their well-developed habits caused them to excel and allowed them to explore more deeply than most other teenagers. Each of the five siblings took an attitude of excellence into their adult lives and pursued wildly different paths as a music therapist, pediatrician, nurse, police officer, and an information technology manager.

Building strong relationships with our children is vital. Expect much, love extravagantly, extend respect, and your fledgling knights will respond. As de Charny wrote, "for the great lord has them in his company and loves, honors, and values them, and they respect him, love, honor, and esteem him for the great valor they see. Then they strive to attain greater heights of prowess."[1] Lead by example. Set the bar high. Remind them of *why* they are to pursue excellence. Then let them take off and fly.

✠ Throwing Down the Gauntlet

Building Habits of Excellence

In the early years, we build foundational habits that will enable our squires to embrace a lifetime of pursuing excellence.

---

1. Geoffroi de Charny, *A Knight's Own Book of Chivalry* (Philadelphia: University of Pennsylvania Press, 2005), p. 59.

✦ Lay out expectations for work contributions around the home. Do not pay your boys for these basic chores. Helping is what a family does to keep things going, and we all do our work well.

✦ Expect excellence for their developmental stage.

- Do the job completely, the first time.
- Don't put it down, put it back. (This was my friend's mantra with her children to create a habit of putting things away throughout the day.)
- Put clothes all the way away.
- Hold your pencil correctly.
- Put toys away correctly.
- Brush teeth correctly.
- Wash your hands. Use soap, clean under fingernails.

✦ Praise going above and beyond the required basics.

✦ Point out a job well done to encourage appropriate pride.

✦ Talk about the concept of going the extra mile. Look at the Code of Chivalry and ask your boys what it would look like to go the extra mile in each of these areas.

✦ When faced with a new task, don't ask, "Can I do this?" Or even "How can I do this?" Learn to ask yourself, "How can I do this well and even better than expected?"

✦ Learn an individual (rather than team) sport or a musical instrument. It provides an excellent opportunity to develop the habits of practice, discipline, and attention to detail. Team sports emphasize the important skill of cooperation, whereas individual sports emphasize personal development.

Expanding on the Foundation

As our children get older they will be able to start thinking about the future, connecting passions with effort and putting the habits of excellence into practice as they set goals to accomplish their dreams.

- ✦ **Set short-term goals.** While my kids are little I set goals several times a year for them in the following areas: spiritual, character, academic, practical living, and physical. I encourage my older boys to take some time to set their own goals. Take your child out for some special time with you and talk about goals he wants to set in each of the areas. Write them down, so he can review.
- ✦ **Set long-term goals.** Ask him what he might want to be vocationally when he grows up.

  - ▪ Challenge him to find out what skills and training one needs to do that work. What can he do *now* to start to prepare for this career?
  - ▪ Find someone in this career who would allow your boy to shadow him or her for a day.
  - ▪ Find a volunteer position in which he could develop skills and see if he truly likes this kind of work.

✠ PART 3

Continuing the
Quest

✝ Chapter 16

Raising Modern-Day Knights Is a Long-Term Quest

These ten commandments [of chivalry] have been the rules and reins of youthful generations, who without them would have been wild and undisciplined. —*Léon Gautier, 1898*

Anticipation swelled as the boys watched the clock, waiting for Daddy to get home. Drumsticks sizzled in the oven and French bread cut in the long white boats of medieval trenchers lay in rows nearby. A pie perched on the counter.

For once, the boys all took baths without complaint because every knight readily agreed to this one bath in his lifetime. Tonight was the grand beginning of the rest of their lives. Tonight, they were to be dubbed knights. After weeks of learning about the knight's Code of Chivalry and daily practice living it out, it was time to make their progress official. Because of their young ages, my husband and I were not sticklers for historical accuracy. Instead, the boys wore their papier–mâché helmets and playsilk capes while holding tightly to their cardboard shields. One boy watched at the window for Dad's arrival while the other two arranged the throne room. Without even allowing their dad to change out of his work clothes, they pleaded with him to start the ceremony. With uncharacteristic reverence and calm, each boy kneeled as their father tapped each shoulder reminding him of the commitment he was making to embody the ideals of a knight.

Over drumsticks, we reminded our boys that this was not the end, but rather just the beginning of the chivalry challenge. They nodded in understanding, indicating that they were ready for the rest of the adventure.

Just this last year, now five years later, Rich and I took time to intentionally revisit this chivalry challenge. While this way of living had become the norm, it was fun to pull out the books again, engage in battle play, and hash out what it looked like to live out the code as older boys, further along in their journey.

We sat around the kitchen table talking as they finished breakfast one morning. Now that they are older these truths need to go deeper. They must own it in a way they did not during their younger years. My baby boy is no longer three, but a busy, kind-hearted eight-year-old. My oldest is headed into the teen years. As we discuss pursuing excellence, we circle back to the beginning and connect the dots. The beginning and the end of the code apply to everything in between. We pursue excellence not to make a better life for ourselves (although it will). We pursue excellence because it is right and it is how we honor God. And God calls us to pursue an all-in lifestyle. As oatmeal bowls are stacked up, they open the Bible and read the charge to them to work heartily for God, not for man. We discuss what that means. Heads nod in understanding. They are all-in. They are to do their best, to be their best because they love God and in turn want to love those around them. Living the knight's life is a life of service—defending, protecting, and caring for others. It is a life they want to live.

✝ Stay Strong

In the days of old, a boy became a page around six or seven years old and did not complete his training until the age of twenty-one. It is important to remember that raising a knight is a long-term quest. Embarking on knight training is not a cute one-time event in our children's lives. It is a lifestyle choice.

Taking up the gauntlet ourselves to raise these boys requires dedication and perseverance. Igniting the imagination and giving boys a vision for what it means to be a modern-day knight is just the beginning. Success requires adopting a mind-set, a firm conviction that you are in this training for the long haul. It is a quest worthy of our time and one that will have repercussions far into the future.

If your boys are anything like mine, they will relish the opportunity to take on this chivalry challenge, knowing that only those brave and determined enough will endure.

In the end they will become the strong leaders of tomorrow who care about others and use their strength and energy to make the world a better place.

"To educate a man in mind and not in morals is to educate a menace to society," Theodore Roosevelt eloquently stated. As we are raising these boys of ours we want this call to captivate their hearts.

We acknowledge there are seasons and stages our boys walk through. As our young squires mature, we release our boys to fight their own battles, even if it means momentary setbacks. It is important that they know we are always there, rooting for them as they internalize and embody this code for themselves. Part of the learning process includes stumbling and sometimes falling along the way as they learn what it means to walk through life. They will come through these experiences stronger and prepared to take on the future.

Along the way, we provide guidance. We embrace our role as rulers of the home domain and prepare them for the domains they will one day rule. And we remember to live by the code ourselves. Robert Fulghum once said, "Don't worry that children never listen to you. Worry that they are always watching you."

Our boys are watching. They want to know what it means to be a boy, what it means to become a man. Our boys take their cues from those closest to them as well as the world around them. Our message needs to overshadow the broken views that our culture propagates about what it means to be a man.

As mothers, we plant the seeds of empathy. We lay the foundation for how a man ought to treat a woman by how we encourage our boys to interact with us in loving, warm, and respectful ways. Mothers bring different perspectives to the table. And our boys need to learn these perspectives to understand and relate to the girls and women they will encounter outside of their homes.

As we acknowledge and celebrate how our boys are different, we can inspire them to grow up to be worthy men—strong and just. One of the best ways we can do this is to honor and respect men, and encourage the relationships our son has with the men in his life.

✠ Recognize the Importance of Male Role Models

The path to knighthood took place under the guidance of a knight. And still today, boys learn to become men from other men. This does not diminish the role a mother plays but rather recognizes the important role men have in their lives. Fathers and mothers are both essential. They each bring something different and unique to the lives of their children. When both men and women are involved in a child's life there is balance.

A boy discovers what it means to be a man by spending time with other men—his father first, but also men in his community. From a young age, my boys became their daddy's shadow, following him around everywhere. Whenever a handyman comes to the house, the boys gather around, asking him about what he is doing and closely observing his work. They adore games of football or basketball out front because sometimes a neighborhood dad joins them. They follow their grandfather around peppering him with questions. During all of this time, they are subconsciously learning the ways of manhood.

Because a child's world is now dominated by women, from their faithful mothers to the predominance of female teachers in school, boys do not get the same interaction with men that they used to receive. For example, in traditional agricultural societies, they would have worked alongside their fathers from young ages. We need to be intentional now more than ever to seek out male role models for our boys, especially if their father is not involved with their lives.

This need is what drove us to find a man to teach our boys piano. This need is also met by playing sports because most coaches are male. Even though I sometimes cringe at the no-nonsense approach, boys need men who tend to bring a tougher man-up approach to their interactions.

✸ Don't Do It Alone: Start a Chivalry Movement

Chivalry played such an important role in history because it was not simply a private pursuit but a communal one. In a world that often sees boys as troublemakers, loud, obnoxious, and unnecessary, we can link arms with other families and begin the rumblings of an entire chivalry movement by shaping the culture of our homes and communities to be a place that welcomes boys in all their boyish exuberance and strength. Support from other parents will help you to stay on track and focused. You will be surprised by how much you can learn from one another. And your competitive boys will enjoy having friends join them on this counterculture quest. We can point them toward the need for men who are strong and valiant, brave and true. And together we can encourage our boys to embody the spirit of a knight.

My friends Dave and Becca sought to do just that with their young boys. They were inspired to raise knights in training but did not want it to be an isolated journey. They recognized the value in bringing alongside fellow knights in training as well as the influences of strong mature knights.

Looking around, they approached a few families with an idea to meet together for training exercises. Every other month, they gather for some kind of adventure. Sometimes it is kayaking at a lake near their home; other times it is as simple as gathering for a big bonfire. In addition, they have a time of intentional discussion about the pursuit of chivalry. In this knight's club, the boys are forming relationships with each other and with the men in the group to spur one another on to standing against injustice and protecting the weak. Each dad takes turns leading the discussion, but with the purpose of igniting the boys to express their ideas and desires.

It takes only one to start a movement. There are families everywhere who are looking at the modern state of boyhood and shaking their heads. They would jump at the chance to join with other like-minded families and create a different future for their boys. Look around you. Find families in your neighborhood, in your schools, and within your churches and religious communities. Invite a few to join you in your quest to make this pursuit of chivalry and the training of your young squires a long-term reality. Meet monthly or every other month—whatever suits your needs and schedules—to take on the chivalry challenge together. Make this fun by engaging the imagination and letting the boys use their bodies. Tell stories of the knights of old, spend time in physical training. This could mean hosting sword-fighting competitions, wrestling matches, or an archery tournament using the ideas in Chapter 5. It does not have to be Pinterest perfect. Your boys care only about the swords anyway. You could plan a service-oriented day on which you go out and help an elderly neighbor or a single mom with yard work. There is no end to the opportunities to get your squires physically involved in their knight training. Focus on one aspect of the Code of Chivalry each time you meet. Discuss how they can live by the code in everyday life and maybe act out a scenario or two. Next time encourage the boys to share their stories of putting the code into practice.

Entering into the world of knights is exciting. Bringing a taste of chivalry into our modern world can fill our boys with passion and purpose for the future. Drawing our friends into the challenge can change our communities and impact the world.

Celebrate boyhood, look forward to the adventure of manhood, and enjoy the journey along the way with your knights-in-the-making!

Knights in Training Resources

Code of Chivalry Poster

Posting the Knight's Code of Chivalry in your home is essential. You can go to www.heatherhaupt.com/knightsintraining to download a printable 8.5 x 11 Code of Chivalry poster to use in your home.

Knights-in-Training Progress for Three- to Seven-Year-Olds

If your young boys enjoy following their progress on a chart, this will help them as they progress through the chivalry challenge. Copies can be printed from www.heatherhaupt .com/knightsintraining.

Chores Kids Can Do by Age

Two to Three Years Old	By Nine Years Old
Put toys in toy basket	Dust and vacuum room
Put shoes in a shoe basket or rack	Hang/fold clean clothes
Put dirty clothes in hamper	Clean bathroom (except toilet/mirror)
Dust with old sock on the hand	Sweep floors
Put silverware and napkins on table	Load dishwasher
Fetch clean diapers; throw soiled diapers away	Cook eggs and toast
	Bake cookies

By Five Years Old	By Eleven Years Old
Put toys away	Put clean sheets on bed
Put folded clothes away	Clean entire bathroom (including toilet/mirror)
Put books on shelf	Wash windows
Make the bed	Clean and wipe countertops/tables
Sort clean silverware	Make a salad
Set table	Mop floors
Clear table	
Wipe down trash cans or doorknobs	
Match socks	

By Seven Years Old	Twelve Years Old and Older
Keep room tidy	Iron
Strip sheets	Do laundry
Empty trash cans	Do simple mending (buttons,
Separate laundry	hems, etc.)
Empty dishwasher	Meal plan
Peel potatoes and carrots	Make grocery list
Fix snacks and simple meals	Grocery shop
(sandwiches, cereal)	Mow lawn
Rake leaves	Wash/vacuum car
Sweep porch	Change oil
	Trim bushes
	Do pool maintenance

Book Recommendations: Adventure, Chivalry, and Character Books

IF YOU CAN GET ONLY FOUR

Hodges, Margaret. *The Kitchen Knight.* Illustrated by Trina Schart Hyman. New York City: Holiday House, 1990.

Hodges, Margaret. *Saint George and the Dragon.* Illustrated by Trina Schart Hyman. New York City: Little, Brown Books for Young Readers, 1990.

O'Brian, Patrick. *The Making of a Knight.* Watertown: Charlesbridge, 1998.

San Souci, Robert. *Young Lancelot.* New York City: Delacorte Press, 1996.

OTHER GREAT MEDIEVAL, KNIGHT, AND CHIVALRY BOOKS

Picture Books

Bishop, Jennie. *Squire and the Scroll.* Anderson: Warner Press, 2004.

Talbott, Hudson, *Excalibur.* New York: Harper Collins, 1996.

Talbott, Hudson. *King Arthur and the Round Table.* New York: Morrow Junior Books, 1995.

Talbott, Hudson, *King Arthur: The Sword and the Stone*. New York City: Books of Wonder, 1991.

Talbott, Hudson, *Lancelot*. New York City: Books of Wonder, 2012.

Tanaka, Shelley. *In the Time of Knights (the Story of William Marshal)*. New York: Disney-Hyperion, 2000.

Chapter Books

Cule, W. E. *The White Knight*. Mount Morris: Lamplighter Publishing, 2003.

Hawke, Ethan. *Rules for a Knight*. New York City: Knopf, 2015.

Audio Dramas

The Dragon and the Raven. Thomson: Heirloom Audio Productions, 2015. The story of King Alfred.

In Freedom's Cause. Thomson: Heirloom Audio Productions, 2014. The story of William Wallace.

Under Drake's Flag. Thomson: Heirloom Audio Productions, 2013. The story of Sir Frances Drake.

Movies

Robin Hood. Walt Disney Studios Home Entertainment, 1973.

The Adventures of Robin Hood. Warner Brothers, 1938. The Errol Flynn version.

The Sword and the Stone. Disney, 1963.

Books to Inspire Further Exploration of the Code of Chivalry

1. Love the Lord Your God with Your Heart, Soul, Mind and Strength

Hunkin, Oliver. *Dangerous Journey*. Grand Rapids: William B. Eerdmans Publishing Company, 1985.

Lloyd-Jones, Sally. *The Jesus Story Book Bible*. Grand Rapids: ZonderKidz, 2007.

Shepherd, Sheri Rose. *His Mighty Warrior: A Treasure Map from the King*. Colorado Springs: Multnomah, 2007.

2. Obey Those in Authority over You

The Gingerbread Man.

Collodi, Carlo. *Pinocchio*. New York: Sterling Children's Books, 2014. Unabridged.

Javernick, Ellen. *What if Everybody Did That?* New York: Two Lions, 2010.

Rosemond, John. *A Family of Value*. Kansas City: Andrews and McNeel, 1995. For parents.

3. Stand against Injustice and Evil

Bible: Book of Proverbs

Biographies about historical heroes who fought against injustice: Patrick Henry, George Washington, Martin Luther King Jr., Frederick Douglass, etc.

Biographies of the recipients of the Congressional Medal of Honor: cmohs.org/recipient-archive.php.

Maybury, Richard J. *Whatever Happened to Justice*. Placerville: Bluestocking Press, 2004. For teens.

Paine, Thomas. *Common Sense*. Mineola: Dover Publications, 1997. For teens.

4. Defend and Protect the Weak

Daly, Niki. *The Herd Boy*. Grand Rapids: Eerdmans Books for Young Readers, 2012.

Ludwig, Trudy. *The Invisible Boy*. New York: Knopf Books for Young Readers, 2013.

Milway, Katie Smith. *One Hen: How One Small Loan Made a Big Difference*. Toronto: Kids Can Press, 2008.

Muth, Jon J. *The Three Questions*. New York: Scholastic Press, 2002.

5. Respect and Honor Women

Jenson, Kristen. *Good Pictures, Bad Pictures: Porn-Proofing Today's Young Kids*. Richland: Glencove Press, 2016. Perfect for any age.

Young, Hal, and Melanie Young. *Love, Honor, and Virtue.* Great
    Waters Press, 2016. Geared for teens and young adult boys.
Protect Young Minds: protectyoungminds.org. For parents.

6. Refrain from Wanton Offense

Beauty and the Beast. Disney, 1991. Lessons in courtesy; the
    scene with Belle and Beast in which he learns to eat properly
    is priceless.
Leaf, Munro. *How to Behave and Why.* New York: Universe,
    1991. For four- to eight-year-olds.
Leaf, Munro. *Manners Can Be Fun.* New York: Universe, 2004.
    For four- to eight-year-olds.
Keller, Laurie. *Do Unto Otters.* New York: Square Fish, 2009. For
    four- to ten-year-olds.
Rowe, Patsy. *Elbows off the Table.* London: New Holland, 2015.
    Readable book on manners geared for seven- to twelve-year-
    olds.
Seven Brides for Seven Brothers. Metro-Goldwyn-Mayer, 1954. A
    hilarious example of how to become a gentleman.

7. Speak the Truth at All Times

Aesop. "The Boy Who Cried Wolf."
Bunting, Eva. *A Day's Work.* New York: HMH Books for Young
    Readers, 1997. A boy learns the importance of truthfulness
    and making things right.
Demi. *The Empty Pot.* New York: Square Fish, 1996.
Earnhardt, Donna W. *Being Frank.* Brooklyn, NY: Flashlight
    Press, 2012.

8. Be Generous and Willing to Share

Aardema, Verna. *Koi and the Kolo Nuts: A Tale from Liberia.*
    New York: Aladdin, 2003.
de Paola, Tomie. *Clown of God.* New York: HMH Books for
    Young Readers, 1978.
Dickens, Charles. *A Christmas Carol.* New York: Dover, 1991.
Toscano, Charles. *Papa's Pastries.* New York: Zonderkidz, 2010.

9. Persevere and Finish the Task at Hand

Bildner, Phil. *The Hallelujah Flight*. New York: G.P. Putnam's Sons Books for Young Readers, 2010.

Biographies of people who overcame setbacks or persevered: Thomas Edison, Abraham Lincoln, Henry Ford, any Olympic athlete.

George, Jean Craighead. *My Side of the Mountain*. New York: Puffin, 2004.

Haupt, Heather. *The Ultimate Guide to Brain Breaks*. Phoenix: Cultivated Lives, 2013. For parents.

Henty, G. A. Novels.

Piper, Watty. *The Little Engine That Could*. New York: Grosset & Dunlap, 2001

Sanderson, Ruth. *The Crystal Mountain*. Northampton, MA: Crocodile Books, 2016.

Spires, Ashley. *The Most Magnificent Thing*. Toronto: Kids Can Press, 2014.

10. Pursue Excellence in All You Do

Bunting, Eva. *A Day's Work*. New York: HMH Books for Young Readers, 1997.

Park, Linda Sue. *A Single Shard*. New York: HMH Books for Young Readers, 2011.

RESOURCES FOR FURTHER READING

Unknown. *The Babees Book: Medieval Manners for the Young*. Trans. Edith Rickert and L. J. Naylor. Cambridge: In Parentheses Publications, 2000.

Unknown, possibly Turold. *Song of Roland*. Trans. Dorothy Sayers. Bungay: Penguin Books, 1957.

Dhuoda. *Handbook for William: A Carolingian Woman's Counsel for Her Son*. Trans. Carol Neel. Washington, D.C.: Catholic University of America Press, 1991.

de Charny, Geoffroi. *A Knight's Own Book of Chivalry*. Trans. Elspeth Kennedy. Philadelphia: University of Pennsylvania Press, 2005.

Eldridge, John. *Wild at Heart: Discovering the Secret of a Man's Soul*. Nashville: Thomas Nelson Publishers, 2001.

Elkind, David. *The Power of Play*. Cambridge: Da Capo Press, 2007.

Rosemond, John. *A Family of Value*. Kansas City: Andrews and McNeel, 1995.

Sax, Leonard. *Boys Adrift*. New York City: Basic Books, 2007.

Sax, Leonard. *Why Gender Matters*. New York City: Broadway Books, 2005.

ACKNOWLEDGMENTS

Books are never created in a vacuum. This one is no exception. I can never thank my family enough for the investment they made in this book. My husband, Rich, is my hero and my rock. He stepped up on the home front so I could get away and write. He kept me going, even when I was tempted to quit. My kids—Alexander, Keegan, Treyton, and Greta—took greater charge of their work at home and were always game to try any new idea that popped into my head for the book. They inspire me.

I am thankful for my mom, Colene Lewis, who believed in this book from the beginning with a fierceness that can only come from mother-love. She gave countless hours of her time coming out to visit, talking about the book, suggesting edits, and, especially in the week before the manuscript was due, swooping in to homeschool the kids and make us the best fried chicken with gravy! Thanks to my dad, Tom Lewis, for modeling to me what courageous and compassionate manhood looks like; you were my first exposure to a modern-day knight. I am thankful for my sister Bethany Miller's brilliant editing help, and for my sister Evie Heller who listened to me talk for hours on end about sections of the book. I am grateful for my always supportive mother-in-law, Vicki Haupt, for her encouragement and assistance with the kids.

I am thankful for friends Jessica Wilhelmsen, Jamie Mehan, Amanda Ippel, Amanda White, Hal and Melanie Young, and Louisa Heller, who shared in the excitement and lent me their stories, and for Matt Chandler, Nancy French, and Annette Economides, who helped me figure out what to expect along the way with this writing journey. Finally, I would love to thank my agent, Chris Park, who walked me through this process with grace and wisdom, and Sara Carder and the rest of the TarcherPerigee team who have been so helpful. Thank you for your enthusiasm and support!

INDEX

Adams, Katherine and Isabelle, 212
adventure, 27–29, 38
Alfred the Great, 71–73, 79
archery, 65–66
Aristotle, 141
Arthur, King, 139–40, 161–62
Augustine, Saint, 77
authority figures, 89–107

battle and weapons, 50–51, 55–58, 62–68, 113, 141–42
    rules of engagement, 61–62
Bennett, William, 119
Boethius, 200
books and reading, 14–15, 19, 22, 34, 46–48, 50, 112–13, 119, 135, 136
    recommendations for, 267–72
boredom, 59–60
boys, 11–24, 25–38, 258–59

Brady, Tom, Jr., 84, 85
Buck, Pearl S., 114
Burke, Edmund, 116
bystander effect, 116–18, 120, 128, 129

character, strength of, 109
Charlemagne, 77–79, 82, 88, 124–25, 199
charting progress, 51, 263
Chesterton, G. K., 48
chivalry, 6–9, 44–49, 258–60
    Code of, ix, 7–8, 43–44, 51–53, 84–86, 249, 253, 260, 263
civility, 12–13
climbing skills, 66
college, 19–20
compassion, 124–30, 135
competition, 32
Coony, Tommy, 113
Couch, Ethan, 16

Covey, Stephen, 35
Crockett, Davy, 112
crudeness, 14–16, 32

De Charny, Geoffroi, 44–45, 79,
    85, 124, 162–63, 239, 248
Dhuoda, 182, 199–200
disagreement, 101–2, 165
Douglass, Frederick, 112
dubbing ceremony, 52, 254
Duckworth, Angela, 219
Durant, Will, 241
Dweck, Carol, 225–26

Edison, Thomas, 220, 225, 242
Eleanor of Aquitaine, 238–39
elders, 99
Eldridge, John, 142
Eliot, T. S., 232
Elkind, David, 60
Emerson, Ralph Waldo, 219
empathy, 17, 32, 112, 129, 135,
    143, 144, 208, 257
engagement, 18–20, 24
entitlement mentality, 16–17
excellence, 237–50, 254–55
expectations, 35–37, 244, 245, 249

failure, 232–33
family culture, 21, 24, 37, 152
fatalism, 5, 10
feelings, 189–90
fists, using, 164–65
Flood, Michael, 147
focus, 231–32, 235, 241
Freed, Richard, 19, 24
Frozen, 23
Fulghum, Robert, 256

Gareth of Orkney, 139–40, 156,
    161–62
Gautier, Léon, 125, 200–201, 253
generosity, 198–216
George, Saint, 74–76, 85, 198–99,
    217–18
gift giving, 211–13, 215
girls, *see* women and girls
God, 6, 71–88, 100, 255
    image of, 80–81, 95, 143
Grandin, Temple, 168–69
grit, 218, 219
Grumney, Jared, 15–16
Guthrum, King, 71–73

habits, 49, 227, 241, 242
Henry, Patrick, 111–12
heroes, 33–35, 37–38, 109–10,
    127, 219
Hodges, Margaret, 75
honesty, 180–97
hope, 85
hospitality, 208–9, 214–15

idealism, 4–5
imagination, 46, 50, 55–61, 255
Imago Dei, 80–81, 95, 143
independence, 20–21
Ippel, Amanda, 221–22

Jacobson, Matthew, 230
Jensen, Kristen, 150
Jobs, Steve, 18
John, King, 82, 200, 239
jousting, 64–65

Kay, Sir, 162
Keefe, Danny, 113

King, Martin Luther, Jr., 112, 119
knaves, 183
knights, 6–7
knight training, 7–9, 41–53
  as long-term quest, 253–61
  physical, 54–70

Lancelot, 76–77, 122–24, 129–30,
  135, 162
leadership, 128
Lego Movie, The, 22–23
Lewis, C. S., 41
Lincoln, Abraham, 162, 165, 220
*Lion, the Witch and the Wardrobe,
  The* (Lewis), 57–58
Lord's Prayer, 87
lying, 181–88, 191–96

manners, 160, 156–79
Marshal, William, 43, 180–82,
  237–39
Mason, Charlotte, 133, 227
McClellan, Megan, 228
McKay, Brett, 30
mealtimes, 166, 170, 174–76
media, 15, 22–24, 60–61, 152
Mehan, Jamie, 133
Middle Ages, 6–8, 43, 46
mind, strength of, 109–10
Mintz, Chris, 113
moral foundation, 109–11
motivation, 32
movement, 30–32, 37, 38, 231–32,
  235
movies, 15, 22–23
Murphy, Audie, 246–47

narcissism, 17, 83, 129–30

obedience, 89–107
offense, refraining from, 159–
  79
outdoors, 61

pages, 41, 42, 92, 113, 165–66
Paine, Thomas, 112, 119
parents, 91–98, 133, 154, 205–6,
  223, 241–42, 257–58
Parker, John, 113
passion, 229, 241, 242, 250
perseverance, 217–36, 240–41
Pew Research Center, 20
Phelps, Michael, 84–85
Pines, Cody, 164–65
play, 46–47, 57, 59, 60, 119, 135,
  136, 229–30
politeness, 12–13
political office, 99–100
pornography, 147–52
potty humor, 14–16
practice, 49, 53, 103, 191, 236,
  240–41
praise, 225–27
protecting the weak, 122–38
prowess, 239–40
purpose, 84–85, 127, 132, 228,
  229, 240

respect, 98–100, 104–5
  for women, 6, 139–58
Richard the Lionheart, 82
risk taking, 28, 32, 37, 114–16
Roland, 43–44, 78, 124
role models, 155–56, 257–58
Roosevelt, Theodore, 171, 256
Rosemond, John, 92–93
rules, 168–70

schools and education, 19, 24
    movement and, 31
Scott, Walter, 191
selfishness, 83, 129, 200–201, 206
self-regulation, 227–28, 236
7 Habits of Highly Effective
    People, The (Covey), 35
sex, 146–47
    innuendo and jokes about,
        14–16, 151
    pornography, 147–52
sharing, 204, 207–8, 211, 214
smiling, 209–11
Smith, Christian, 203
Song of Roland, The, 43–44, 78,
    124
Spires, Jasper, 117
squires, 41–42, 92, 152, 165–66,
    256
    work of, 68–70
stability, 126–27
standing against injustice, 108–21
Story of Philosophy, The (Durant),
    241
strength, 109–10, 128–30, 159
    physical, 29–30, 38, 110, 128,
        132, 135, 144
Sutherland, Kevin, 116–17
swords, 62–64

Talwar, Victoria, 183
teachers, 98–99
technology, 18–19
television, 15, 22, 23
throwing down the gauntlet, 9
    becoming a gentleman, 156–58
    being generous, 213–16
    growing habits of obedience
        and loyalty, 103–7

not giving offense, 172–79
passing on our faith, 86–88
perseverance, 233–36
protecting the weak, 136–38
pursuing excellence, 248–50
speaking truth, 194–97
standing against injustice,
    118–21
time, 60
truth, 180–97
Turansky, Scott, 190–91
Tutu, Desmond, 81
Twenge, Jean M., 129

Ungar, Michael, 115

video games, 22, 24
virtue, 83–84, 141, 148
Voskamp, Ann, 146

Washington, George, 112
weapons, see battle and weapons
Webster, Daniel, 111
Welch, Kristen, 16–17
White, Amanda, 211–12
"why," knowing, 32–33, 94–95
women and girls, 6, 32, 126,
    139–58, 228–29
    see also sex
words, using, 163, 188–89, 195
work, 20, 68–70, 107, 230,
    242–44, 249
    chores by age, 264–65
    inspecting, 97–98, 243–44
wrestling, 67–68

Young, Hal and Melanie, 147–48,
    230